Dare to Make a Difference?

The story of Pabloo, a courageous People Manager in a corporate setting who dares to make a difference!

Krishnan Bangarusamy

ISBN 979-8-88935-813-8

Book Dedication

I wanted to thank all the HR leaders and Academians from whom I have borrowed the learnings, concepts, and frameworks. My part is just a humble effort in bringing it all together. I dedicate this book to my brave nephew, Pabloo, who stands tall in spite of the challenges life throws at him.

Krishnan Bangarusamy

Book Endorsements

"Dare to Make a Difference is a captivating and inspiring story that will leave readers feeling empowered to make a difference in their teams and companies, starting now. Krishnan has written an exceptional book for anyone seeking inspiration and guidance in becoming a transformational leader who values people, ethics, and synergy."

Dr. Marshall Goldsmith,
Dr. Marshall Goldsmith is the Thinkers50 #1 Executive Coach and New York Times bestselling author of The Earned Life, Triggers, and What Got You Here Won't Get You There.

Many studies offer insights on people as at the heart of an organization. This well researched and cleverly written book turns these insights into actions with Pabloo as he develops his people. Krishnan offers a relevant look into how managing people actually happens.

Dave Ulrich, Father of Modern HR,
Rensis Likert Professor of Business, University of Michigan,
Partner, The RBL Group.

'This book truly captures the value of HR as a profession. The narration is engaging, creative, unique, and yet compelling! It powerfully reaches proven self-development and people management techniques in an appealing way to Gen Y and Z. I love the way the author uses the story of Pabloo to engage the reader through the learning process. This book will inspire you to stay committed to your professional pursuits for a rewarding career working with people. Congratulations Krishnan, You are making a difference!'

Ester Martinez,
People Matters,
CEO & Editor-in-Chief.

Contents

Preface of the Book...9

Foreword 1...11

Foreword 2...13

Foreword 3...17

Introduction 19

1. Celebrations!...23
2. Hello Budapest – The First Evening.....................................27
3. The Second Evening 34
4. Mid-Night Ice Cream and Rains..40
5. The Third Afternoon..46
6. The Millennials 51
7. Questions Galore..57
8. Welcome Home..66
9. A People Conversation between a Baby Boomer, Gen X, and Gen Y - Part 1...73
10. A People Conversation between a Baby Boomer, Gen X and Gen Y - Part 2...86
11. A People Conversation between a Baby Boomer, Gen X and Gen Y - Part 3...98
12. The Fourth Day - A Discussion with the Ceo 111
13. Hello Slovakia 117
14. The Last Day 123
15. Slide 1: Make No Mistake, Small is the New Big..................131

16. Slide 2: Technology and Innovation 136

17. Slide 3: Change and the Speed of Change 141

18. Slide 4: Motivation and Communication 147

19. Slide 5: Leadership 154

20. Slide 6: People Practices 160

21. The Last Slide: Do We Dare to Make a Difference? 173

Bibliography *179*

Preface of the Book

Managing and leading people is central to the success of any winning organization. It is projected that the Millennials or the Gen Y population (born between the 1980s and late 90s) in India will cross 50% of the working population by 2025. With close to 40% of our population in the age group between 13 and 35, the younger generation is poised to lead our country on the path of success. Morgan Stanley report reveals that India will be a serious contender for becoming the third-largest economy by 2030!

However, these projections do not alter the reality that we are facing. It is claimed that more than a third of management pass-outs need employability skills. Across many organizations, most young working professionals and managers are driven by factors that add no self-meaning or purpose. They do what they have been asked to do without being able to see the bigger picture and purpose. Often they are less inspired and eventually, they lose fizz. The high turnover in this working population is a perfect example that paints the relationship of this workforce with organizations. The need is more than ever to groom young leaders!

This is the story of Pabloo, a courageous People Manager in a corporate setting who dares to make a difference! Driven by his firm belief that 'People make all the difference,' he is not intimidated by hierarchy, resistance to change, organizational culture, or any other social or political factor coming his way as a potential derailer. He refuses to be an ordinary manager and dons multiple hats to bring all the stakeholders together to build a profitable organization driven by synergy, values, and ethics.

The book captures the imagination of the readers in a European setting, and it follows Pabloo's inspirational way of dealing with organizational challenges and real-time people issues, including,

- How do people managers drive a sense of meaning into their work and motivate their team for peak performance and achieve excellence?
- How do we translate proven talent frameworks into best people practices for the desired organizational results?
- How does every action of a determined and committed individual have a positive impact that adds value to the growth of the organization, community, and the nation's economy?

In this journey, he also coaches upcoming professionals and management students to overcome their inhibitions, channel their work energy into outcomes, and achieve their dream goals.

Simply put, Pabloo Dares to Make a Difference!

Krishnan Bangarusamy

Foreword 1

My personal belief is that every person has the ability to do things that they believed they were incapable of, until by a stroke of luck, or circumstances, they discovered themselves at their successful best. The driving belief is that every human being has the potential to do remarkable things, and have the ability to tap that potential. Put this into a collective as in a team, or an organisation, it would be remarkable to see the outcome. So, how does one find out the magic formula or the magic potion that can create this magic again and again, that they can realize their dreams? One does not have to look far.

When the author Krish reached out to me with his manuscript I was keen to write in a few lines as a forward.

In an unusual but exciting way, he has taken an approach of reaching the time-tested and proven concepts and frameworks of management in an unique way to the readers (Gen Y and Gen Z) by combining management theory with fiction. As an HR practitioner, he professes the value of Human Resources as a Profession. I know it is only too valid in my career spanning more than four decades in this field. Human Resources has the power and ability to influence and positively impact every individual's life. In many ways, People managers are the heroes of the management world, and I'm glad this book brings out those elements and attributes of these humble and authentic human beings.

The present and the future of the world of work belong to the Gen Y and Z workforce. I'm confident this book will inspire these readers to 'Make a difference' to individuals, groups, organizations, and the community. To many who wish to find out the magic ingredients of success, this book is a recommended read. Sometimes, the most complicated framework is a simple set of to dos. Read on !!

Nathan SV,
National President, NHRDN, India, 2021-23.

Foreword 2

Working with organizations for more than two decades has assured me that no matter where you work, what role you have, and how much you are paid – unless you are empathetic, you can never make a change.

However, change is the only thing constant in our lives and the most basic thing without which progress cannot take place.

In the digital era, to match the pace of change, it is often emphasized to prioritize data analytics and algorithms. What cannot be ignored is that each data point is actually a living breathing human. Their ambitions in life extend beyond the list of career objectives and their perspectives can seem out of place in the corporate world. The search and struggle to align their own passion with the purpose of the organization can make them feel stagnant and discouraged from taking initiative.

This is the point where the decline in performance, engagement and satisfaction begins and also where the stage is set for experimentation and innovation. It is the leader who has to make the choice. Should the tried and tested methods be continued or is it the lack of system upgrades that are creating the gap? Will reducing human effort by automating database management systems share the burden of the workforce? These questions can linger in the mind of the leader.

In such situations, one thing that needs to be remembered is that although times will change, technology will advance and trends will come and go, humans will remain the entities that drive success.

A viewpoint that considers employees more than metrics and performance appraisals allows them to grow as well as make the workplace community more human. Collective growth is the secret behind the success of an organization and it begins with acknowledging the voice of every individual at work – from interns to veterans.

Talk to the people, ask them what they want and where the change needs to happen. Then give them the solution – give them what they need.

Valuing and validating each diverse voice also becomes more important now that the workforce has multiple generations working together. The prejudices in the minds of the people can become the result of clashes and hamper both the bonds and the business. Here, again – human leadership can not only solve problems but support innovation, the one thing that keeps the spark and the businesses alive.

This is what Krishnan has recognized and thus, has donned multiple hats throughout his more than a decade on the journey – of a coach, a challenger, a mentor and an influencer. The role of a leader is simple and straightforward while the responsibilities are numerous and multi-layered. He has identified the need and resourcefulness of humans – not only for the organization but for their own growth. Both of us being associated with ICF get to share the enlightening experiences of learning and unlearning what we know and understand about leadership.

I see in his published book the reflection of similar wisdom. This book is a deep dive into those challenges and the discovery of their solutions.

With the story of Pabloo, he has managed to explain and elaborate on what prioritizing humans can do to make an impact. Sketches and humour have enhanced such a serious subject while making it more creative and engaging. The use of acronyms and their meaningful breakdown have made it easier to grasp the complex power and responsibility behind them. We know T&C as terms and conditions but the interesting twist that Krishnan has given is something I have never come across: trust and change.

Human resources, social psychology, emotional intelligence, the global economy or business strategy — he has researched leadership from every domain to mindfully pick theories, formulae and examples to back his claims. His idea to combine science and spirituality to reach harmony between the mind and the soul is something I personally agree with. Without forgetting his ethical values and Indian roots, he has reestablished the purpose of progress – unity in diversity.

From the bottom to the top, on the front to the back end, and at the core to the surface, it's humans who make businesses develop and organizations shine — human leadership can become the wind under their wings. Krishnan has devised solutions in a human way and all of us can utilize this guidance to contribute to the human world, both inside and outside of the organization.

Muniinder K Anand,
Managing Director – India, South Asia & Global Support Center,
Center for Creative Leadership.

Foreword 3

Greetings!

I am pleased to introduce you to "Dare to Make a Difference" by the highly accomplished talent management expert and TMI alumnus Krishnan Bangarusamy. With a dedication to objectivity and information sharing that has left an indelible mark on the talent management community for the last few years, Krishnan's latest work is a must-read for anyone seeking to understand the theoretical foundations of talent management.

The book covers an impressive array of 100 theories, concepts, and ideas closely related to human resource management. It is a comprehensive guide that offers insights into talent management principles and methods that can positively impact the world.

Throughout the pages of his book, Krishnan's acute insights into human psychology and the far-reaching effects of talent management on the workforce are evident. He expertly uses storytelling and discussion to explain complex ideas clearly and elegantly. Furthermore, he shows utmost respect for his readers and subjects.

I firmly believe that knowledge can bring about transformation, and I am confident that readers of "Dare to Make a Difference" will gain valuable insights from Krishnan's expertise and empathy. I encourage everyone to approach this book with an open mind and heart; it will serve as a valuable resource for personal and professional growth.

Balabhadra Pattnaik,
GTML™,
Fellow of Talent Management Institute,
Head - Organization Development,
Al Jazeera Media Network.

Introduction

Gurumurthy Kalyanaram

Krishnan Bangarusamy has produced an imaginative manuscript on change, motivation, and leadership. It is imaginative for many reasons. It is conversational. It is catechistic. It is evidence-based. It is practical. It is a pattern – a daily happening and insight. The insights are boldly labeled as Slides.

The rhetorical question, "Do we dare to make a difference?" is foundational to the form of change that we may espouse, evoke, and seek and the form of leadership we are likely to demonstrate, embrace and encourage. Making a difference requires purposeful intent and a willingness to suffer and sacrifice for the larger cause.

It is my empirical observation that contingency theory of leadership has the most explanatory power in explaining and describing impactful leadership.

For instance, let's look at Mahatma Gandhi. Mahatma Gandhi was a product of his times. Non-violence was championed by Gopal Krishna Gokhale decades before the arrival of Gandhi in India in 1916 from South Africa. But in 1916 India was poised to be empathetic to calls for autonomy and independence – the country had been primed for decades. Serendipitously, Rabindranath Tagore who had won Nobel Prize in 1913 (first Nobelist from India) and who was considered saintly and spiritual simply said, "The Mahatma is coming," as Gandhi was sailing to India. That immediately raised the stature of Gandhi. It was confluence of many elements including Gandhi's personal attributes that produced Gandhi's leadership.

Similar compelling arguments are apposite for Mikhail Gorbachev and Nelson Mandela. After decades of stifled societal expression and stagnant economy, and successive quick deaths of three leaders – Leonid Brezhnev, Yuri Andropov and Konstantin Chernenko – the Soviet Union was ready for a change and for a younger leader in 1985. Thus was Mikhail Gorbachev's leadership was born. In South Africa, after 27 years of incarceration and a global campaign and condemnation of apartheid, South Africa was ready for change in 1990. Nelson Mandela was released, and he formed a partnership with the Whites to forge a new identity for South Africa. In each of these cases, it is contingent circumstances that produced a transformational leadership.

Of course, we must recognize that while contingency theory of leadership is a powerful framework to describe, it is definitionally too complex and contextual to be parsimonious and useful in a priori predictions.

Apart from leadership and related topics, I am delighted to see a discussion of Technology and Innovation also in the context of change, motivation, and leadership.

Adoption and diffusion of technology is a critical element of change. It has always been. Technology may be small or big; incremental or radical; hi-tech or low-tech. For instance, new approaches to irrigation and/or agriculture or conserving soil and/or water or personal and/or professional communication or diagnostic and/or therapeutic medicine are all examples of technologies. We know that India has successfully adopted and diffused technologies in several areas for the good of the larger society. Such as in producing the green revolution or the white revolution or eye health (including mass and efficient Cataract surgeries.)

We know that technology and innovation have been the most impactful catalytic elements in the sustained prosperity of the United States. Nobelist Robert Solow has demonstrated empirically that technology is a very important input into productivity and prosperity.

I did enjoy the implications of the title, "Small is the new Big." Of course, it is. Nanoscience, nanomaterials, nanotechnologies. Miniaturization. This is also applicable to productive work-habits and leadership components – small steps together compose a big leap cumulatively. Incrementalism cumulates to substantiality. That's what path dependence speaks to. Where you begin is where you end because where you begin often determines the next step, and the second step determines the third, and thus the path dependence originates.

Organically, the insights directly and derivatively derived from "Small is the new Big" impact the pace of desirable and plausible change. So, the section on the Speed of Change fits in so seamlessly.

Overall, this manuscript is worthy of our review. It is fun, it is educational, it is insightful, it is practical. Importantly, the manuscript is also grounded in scholarly and practical intellectual output. What I like about this manuscript is that Bangaruswamy is a person of practice who has produced a manuscript grounded in theory and empirics.

Dr. Gurumurthy Kalyanaram, a doctoral alumnus of Massachusetts Institute of Technology and an alumnus of Woodrow Wilson Center for International Scholars, has served and continues to serve as an advisor, dean, professor, and consultant globally. Currently, he is also the Educational Counselor at MIT.

Celebrations!

C heers! Chirped Pabloo, as he enjoyed the good company and the vibrant atmosphere. He looked around the dining hall and saw all his colleagues in an animated conversation. It was good to see them all celebrating. 'Well, not bad for a bunch that was on a flight journey for close to 10 hours,' murmured Pabloo. As he looked further, he saw the CEO talking to his direct reports. They all seem to be engaged in some serious discussion. 'Must be discussing something strategic', thought Pabloo. The occasion was the first day of the annual meet dinner party celebrating the success of the previous year's organizational goals. Actually, it was a little more than a dinner party; it is a six days event in Budapest, Hungary, celebrating the grand success, which is usually arranged only for senior management folks for about 20 members. Pabloo was excited to be part of this event but was also wondering What's next..!

'Pabloo, come and join us' a voice echoed.

'Coming, chief!' answered Pabloo as he walked towards the group.

It was a four member group including the CEO, Mr. Singh, a gentleman in his mid-fifties with the company's functional heads - Strategy, Finance and Sales. Singh is a successful businessman. He started this

Product based company with a handful of employees about 7 years ago in Bangalore, India, and is currently enjoying the success of this venture with an 800+ workforce. A determined and balanced leader, his clear focus on the results has been his forte.

'What's in store?' thought Pabloo as he walked across the lavish dinner spreads on the tables in the room.

'Tell us Pabloo, what are your viewpoints regarding the expansion of our Operations into a couple of more centers, at least one, to begin with? We thought that we wanted to do this from a business continuity standpoint and as an HR manager your opinion matters!'

Every opportunity is to make an impression, thought Pabloo and mentioned, 'Great! It's just about time we did it. I can put something together and run it across this group.'

'You do that. We all seem to be in agreement and we wanted to go for it for quite a long time.'

Pabloo heard all of them giving their viewpoints. it was interesting to note that local talent availability and employability was the main point to be discussed among all the leaders. 'Wow!' thought Pabloo, HR has come a long way from its humble beginnings to the most debatable topic among the leadership.

'Remember, what has worked well for us all this while need not necessarily work for us now especially, in the context of the new location' cautioned Singh to the group. 'Pabloo, you need to consider all factors from a people aspect before you send this presentation,' he further added.

'Pabloo, come and join us'

Singh's confidence in Pabloo has always been high. Pabloo brings 12 years of work experience in Human Resources and has been enjoying his success in this organization for over 3 years now. The company has grown approximately 200% year on year in the last two years and Pabloo has been enjoying the limelight from a talent resource standpoint. But the time has come to make a big move, thought Pabloo. He has been waiting for a real opportunity to make a true contribution to the business through the field of HR. But in his experience, he has always seen business priorities taking over HR priorities. Maybe it is time that he made an impression considering the interest of all the stakeholders, most importantly, its employees for sustainable business performance through best HR practices.

Pabloo continued enjoying the dinner party but at the back of his mind, his real excitement was that of the new center and the difference he can make.

Around 10:00 PM local time, things seem to be hitting high. As it happens at every party, people were extra affectionate and loving, thanks to social drinking. Pabloo checked his watch and wondered what he, a tea lover is doing here amidst a bunch of whiskey and scotch drinkers. He was slowly losing interest in that room, but then a gentle breeze caught his attention. It seems to be coming from a sit-out area of the restaurant. As he stepped out to enjoy the night breeze, he was blown away seeing the beautiful landscape of Budapest from the 10th-floor restaurant. Just below him was the lovely Danube River with boat cruises. It was one of the most beautiful cities he had visited. It was picturesque with a combination of medieval and modern buildings. 'Magical!' murmured Pabloo and decided to take a walk by the river.

He was pretty excited about the new business location that was discussed, and time off in another country would be an excellent way to put things together. Pabloo slowly made his way back to the dining hall and wanted to sneak out. As he came, he saw no reason to do that, as his colleagues were in their own world. Slightly smiling at whomever he saw, he made his way out to the lobby of the restaurant and eventually to the riverside.

Hello Budapest – The First Evening

Walking by the river Danuabe, he experienced a different feeling and after some time, found a nice spot by the river for a sit-out. He sat there taking a deep breath and continued to gaze at the river. Just then, he noticed another person who was sitting next to him. A well-built gentleman in his 50s also seemed to enjoy the pleasant evening. Pabloo just smiled at him.

'Good evening, which country are you from?' said the other person.

Pabloo initially hesitated but then mentioned 'I'm from Bangalore, India,' and smiled gently.

'India…great! Welcome to Budapest, the most beautiful city in the world.'

Pabloo was pleasantly surprised by such a warm welcome from a stranger. Instantly he mentioned 'Second most beautiful city after Bangalore', and both exchanged smiles. There was something about this stranger, thought Pabloo, he certainly seemed to be an energetic person.

'So, do you live in Budapest?'

'Oh yes! My origin is from the other part of the town – Pest, but it does not really matter as it is all united as Budapest' mentioned the stranger. 'By the way I am Michael!' he mentioned.

'Nice meeting you Michael, I'm Pabloo!' and they shook hands.

'Michael, how come you can speak English? I was told the local dialect here is Hungarian,' asked Pabloo.

'That is correct; I picked it from my young years. I'm a teacher by profession and a principal at the local university here in Budapest. I was an English teacher before becoming the local college principal. Also, I travel frequently to other countries and this language helps.'

'So, is this your first visit to Hungary?'

'It is my first visit to anywhere in Europe. I have come along with my office's senior management folks for an annual meeting. We are here for 6 days celebrating the success of our last year's organizational achievements.'

'Great! Sounds exciting! Are you a salesperson?'

'No, I'm a people person.' smiled Pabloo. 'I manage the Human Resources of the company. Our company is a product-based company with over 800 employees on our payroll. I take care of people-oriented organizational activities.'

'Wow! Sounds like an exciting role!'

'Definitely, yet it is also challenging! You see, what's important in this role is to strike a balance between the management and its employees.'

'...And how do you do that?'

Pabloo was surprised as he was not expecting the question, 'Well, it has its own course Michael, many aspects have to be considered and I'm not sure if I can state all of it now.'

Michael smiled and said, 'Well, the night is still young, my friend. See, the reason for my inquisitiveness is that my daughter works in Human Resources. She has a total experience of 5 years in this field and I enjoy conversations that I have with her related to her work. We respect and value each other's opinions about her day-to-day work in HR. Lately, she has been complaining the work is getting more complicated with people issues. Though she loves her profession because of this reason, she is planning to move out of HR. I would definitely get benefitted from your input and for all you know, it can make a difference to the career of my daughter.'

Wow, to meet a stranger in another country and share things is a good thing but to meet someone to whom you can make a difference is a great thing, thought Pabloo, and said 'I will certainly give my input Michael and would be happy if it adds value at some level to your daughter and you. You see, when I mentioned striking a balance, employees as individuals can have many aspirations and expectations. On the other hand, the management has its own priorities and business interest. It is up to HR to ensure a balance between these two for sustainable organizational performance considering the interest of both parties. To begin with, if I have to say how we do that, Psychological contracting[1] is one way to set this expectation.

'Psychological contracting?, You mean to say they go through some sort of psychological evaluation?'

Pabloo quickly responded, 'Let me explain this in a better way. You see, there is no definitive explanation of the psychological contract. But basically, it refers to the set of beliefs individuals hold related to promises made for themselves for their common interests. For employees, it is concerned with the individual's subjective beliefs, and for employers, the expectations they provide employees within the wage-work bargain. Importantly, since psychological contracts represent differences in the ways management and workers interpret promises and commitments with each other, both parties have differences regarding specific terms of this contract. A major feature of the psychological contract is the concept of mutuality. This is usually established at the time of joining. From employee relations, it is concerned with employees'

---

[1] David E. Guest, Neil Conway (2002), Human Resource Management Journal. Wiley Online Library.'

subjective beliefs, shaped by the organization, in relation to its role as an employer. It is also concerned with the organization's subject belief in relation to the individual. It is important to note that both parties can have different belief systems. However, as mentioned earlier, the basic feature of Psychological contracting is the concept of mutuality.'

Michael said, 'Wow, I did not know there was so much depth to it. That being said, I am still curious to know how you deal with the balancing part.'

'Oh yes, this is where we come into the role. As HR professionals, we approach Psychological contracting in two ways to strike a balance. The first one is through Transactional, a defined and short-term approach of what is agreed to and what is achieved. Usually, it is based on the deal or the contract of completing the job and taking the pay. The second one is more long-term and is the Relational approach, which is based on mutual trust and respect. On one end, the employer offers job, promotion prospects, training and development. On the other hand the employee reciprocates the goodwill by commitment, loyalty, etc. As you would agree, we take the long-term relational approach and this sometimes can lead to a mismatch in mutual expectation and eventually a difference of opinion and our role would be to match the mutual expectation.'

'But why bother to do this Pabloo? Wouldn't it be much simpler to follow the transactional approach? I mean it is black and white and more defined.' mentioned Michael sounding practical.

'I agree Michael, It might have lesser uncertainty but as HR professionals, one of the key tasks for us is to build a credible brand, a preferred employer of choice, and for that, we usually look to strategize and take an approach that is relational such as RBVF, an inside out strategy.'

'RBVF? Inside out? Strategy? Wow! It all sounds like missile launch terms, Are you preparing them for war?' quipped Michael.

'There is a huge science behind HR'

'There is a huge science behind HR. You see, RBVF, a resource-based view of the firm, is an HR people strategy[2]. It is called an Inside out strategy because it considers the internal resources of the firm as a starting point in understanding the successful performance of the organization. It is considered a significant strategy as it leads to change from the earlier outside-in approach, which is more focused on the external environment for the strategy, for example, Competition.' Pabloo noticed Michael's puzzled expression and asked, 'Are you with me, Michael?'

'Yes, Potato, Patato!' smiled Michael.

Pabloo quickly added, 'On the contrary, it is more than a minor detail. You see, an Inside-out approach such as RBVF considers the internal

---

[2]   Boxall, P and Purcell, J (2003), *Strategic Human Resource Management*, Palgrave Macmillan, Basingstoke.

resources as the starting point to lead to questions to strategize, unlike a traditional outside-in strategy which is shaped by market factors. Let me try and explain this better. When I say a mobile phone, which brand comes to your name and why?'

'Apple comes to my mind. The reason maybe it is a standard apart?' Michael answered quickly.

'Exactly, it is because the talents behind Apple's product are heterogeneous and Immobile; those are the two key assumptions in an RBVF strategy. The first is that organizational skills, capabilities, and other resources differ from company to company. This means every organization is diverse yet unique. The second assumption is that resources are not mobile and do not move from company to company, at least in the short run. Based on these two assumptions, an RBVF philosophy proves that every organization has a unique bundle of assets, including human assets. The access to these and the ability to use them effectively gives them a competitive advantage. Therefore, the key aspect of this is to develop the internal human capital, not just the behavioral aspect but also the skills, knowledge and ability. Here is where HR plays a role in building the internal human capital and retaining these talents.'

'I understand developing the human capital part, but what is the guarantee of retaining them, Pabloo?'

'I agree Michael, after all, people have their own free will and choices, but HR here with the good support of the management can add value by bringing in best practices and making the organization - An Employer of Choice' explained Pabloo.

'hmm...It is interesting, but I bet it is a tough task!'

Pabloo added, 'It is a challenging task but it is a real opportunity for the HR to make an impact and positive impression'.

Michael immediately asked another question 'And I'm curious to know about the best practices.'

Just when Pabloo was about to respond, his watch beeped and he quipped 'Wow! I did not realize it was 11 PM already'

'Oh really? Even I did not realize' said Michael.

'It only goes to show, Time is agnostic to a good conversation and a pleasant evening' Pabloo said.

'I agree! In fact, I find it to be interesting and insightful to the ways of Human Resources. If it is not too much to ask, maybe we can continue this conversation tomorrow? I'm absolutely confident it is making a difference for me in the way I look at HR and it will mean a lot to my daughter's career ambition. Maybe we can catch up tomorrow if you are free?'

'I will be happy to meet you Michael. Say by 9 PM, will it work?'

'Absolutely,' said Michael.

'Do you have a number so that I can reach out to you?'

'I never carry a mobile but I will be on time. Maybe you can give me your number just in case.'

Pabloo shared his number and Michael agreed to reach him in case of any change in plan. After quickly acknowledging and thanking each other for the time spent, they shook hands and parted ways. As Pabloo walked toward the hotel by the side of the river, he noticed the city was still buzzing with lights. For some reason, he was feeling very content full and happy. Maybe because of the conversation he had with Michael or the beautiful surrounding.

The Second Evening

It was such a beautiful day as Pabloo enjoyed the sightseeing in Budapest. The first visit was to Buda Castle. Popularly known as the Royal Castle, it was a beautiful 17th-century medieval marvel. Now, it is declared as Budapest's world heritage site. Pabloo and his entire team were in awe of this magnificent place and were fully thrilled. In the afternoon they all enjoyed the local cuisine and then made their way to Fisherman's bastion. Again, another beautifully constructed neo-gothic style seven towers marvel. The highlight of this fisherman's bastion is the terrace from where you get a panoramic view of the river Danube. As Pabloo was gazing at the river, the previous night's meeting with Michael came up to his mind. It was around 4 pm as he looked at his watch. Actually, Pabloo was a little excited and was looking forward to the meeting in the evening.

'Let's face it, it is not often one gets an opportunity to make an impression on a stranger in a different continent' thought Pabloo. Just a quarter to 9 PM, Pabloo finished his dinner and made his way to the spot for the agreed meet-up with Michael.

It was exactly 9 PM and Pabloo respects the time and always ensures to practice being on time. As he started to gaze at the river, he saw cruise boats ferrying people. He got more excited as his colleagues and he are scheduled to take the cruise on the last day of their stay. It was 9.15 PM and Pabloo checked his mobile to see if Michael left any message for him. He noticed a lot of WhatsApp unread messages but none from Michael. It was 9.30 PM and Pabloo was still waiting for Michael.

'Well, so much for the difference' thought Pabloo. As he was just about to leave, he noticed a girl coming from the same direction. She was well dressed and must be in her mid-twenties. She seemed to be looking around both ways as she walked a little closer to the spot. Pabloo just sat there for a minute more as he observed her walking towards him. At first, Pabloo thought she is looking for a place to sit to enjoy the evening by the riverside. But it came as a surprise to him when she smiled at him while walking straight towards him. Pabloo too smiled back and stood up to leave. By that time, the girl was right in front of him and asked, 'Where do you think you are leaving Pabloo?'

'Where do you think you are leaving Pabloo?'

Pabloo was shocked and wondered what was happening. How she knows his name. He was short of words and just kept looking at her.

She then again said, 'Relax! I am Rachel, Michael's daughter!'

Pabloo stood still and it took him 10 seconds to connect things and expressed 'Wow, I never imagined that coming!'.

'Sorry I did not mean to scare you! And by the way, you can call me Rachel.'

'Well Rachel, for a moment you left me to feel a little more than that. How on earth do you know that I'm Pabloo?'

'Well honestly, it is no brainer Pabloo, you and my father agreed to meet here in this spot. He did describe your features to some extent and you are the only foreigner here, so...'

They don't call these youngsters 'millennials' without a reason, thought Pabloo. They are smart, they are fast, and most importantly, naturally comfortable the way they are.

'Is Rachel bothering you much', another voice echoed. As Pabloo turned around, it was Michael standing and passing a warm smile greeting Pabloo. 'Hello Michael, I thought you would not be able to make it today and just about the time I thought of leaving, Rachel marched in and introduced herself', said Pabloo.

'Boy, I am glad! Also please accept my apologies; we had to fix a flat tire on our way here. Even had you left, I would have reached you on your mobile', explained Michael. 'Thanks for mentioning Michael, I was also looking forward to meeting you today' mentioned Pabloo. He looked at his daughter and said 'Rachel, your dad mentioned you in our conversation yesterday, I'm happy to meet a fellow HR person'.

'Like-wise Pabloo!' mentioned Rachel. 'I work in a manufacturing unit here in Budapest as an employee relations senior officer'. She further added 'My dad spoke about you a lot through the course of the day, and I requested him to join you guys here today. I should say, you have had an impression on him with your RBVF, psychological contracting, inside out and outside in concepts, He is fascinated!'

'She is right in saying that and I'm looking forward to hearing your ideas on the best practices that we were speaking about yesterday' mentioned Michael.

Pabloo's eyes lit up, 'Well, it's not my concept, to be honest. These are globally tested and accepted concepts designed by some of the finest HR leaders. On the best practices, one of the popular HR models is the Harvard Business Model[3]. Known as a soft HRM practice, it considers situational factors and the interest of the stakeholders for its HR policies and outcomes. Usually, it is aimed at long-term consequences. Naturally, HR plays a key role in its policies and practice of effective selection, good appraisal, rewards and recognition, training and development, flexibility and participation and employee involvement. Another popular best practice model is an AMO model[4] for high-performance work systems. AMO stands for Ability, Motivation and Opportunity. Again, HR plays a key role in all three aspects. Rachel acknowledged it by stating ' it rings a bell in my mind, I remember reading about this in my Master's in Human Resources'. Pabloo looked at Michael and quickly read his expression, 'I know it all sounds theoretical Michael, let me give you some examples and try to explain this in a better way'

'Yes sure, that will help' mentioned Michael.

'Practically, these are bundles of HR practices that enhance business performance in all organizations, irrespective of the product markets, technology and other contingent factors affecting them. This great performance and competitive edge are gained through improved employee attitudes and behaviors, lower levels of absenteeism and labor turnover, and higher levels of productivity, quality and customer service. Essentially all of these are achieved by putting people first, the importance of human equation in organization', said Pabloo. 'Human

---

[3] Beer, M., et al. (1985). Managing human assets. Personnel Administrator, 30(3), 74–81.

[4] Purcell, J., Kinnie, N., Hutchinson, S., Rayton, B., & Swart, J. (2003). Understanding the people and performance link: Unlocking the black box. London: CIPD.

equation?' asked Michael puzzled. 'Yes, Human Equation[5]. These are best practices that are built around **7** components. They are:

Employment Security and Internal Labor Market – This underpins the other six practices. The basic agreement is you cannot ask the employee to work hard with commitment without some expectation of job security and future career.

Selective Hiring and Sophisticated Selection – Recruiting and retaining the talented workforce.

Extensive Training Learning and Development – Continuous investment in Leadership and Development.

Employee Involvement, Information Sharing and Worker Voice – A view on open and transparent communication about financial matters, strategy and operational problems ensures trust in the organization, increases employee engagement and promotes suggestions to improve the overall performance of the organization.

Self-Managed Teams/Team Working – Teamwork is seen as a solution to operational problems.

High Compensation Contingent Upon Performance – Pay for performance culture and generally higher compensation than the average industry.

Reduction of Status Differentials/Harmonization – To build an 'open' management culture and break artificial barriers among different groups of staff.

'So, there are 7 then Pabloo, I thought it was one human equation' acknowledged Michael. Pabloo quickly responded, 'It is only one Michael, the seven components are part of that single human equation. The idea was presented by the brilliant Jeffrey Pfeffer in his book 'The human

---

[5] Pfeffer,J (1998) The Human Equation: Building Profits by Putting People First, Harvard Business School Press.

equation – Building profits by putting people first'. Pfeffer has brilliantly put forward alternate ways to conventional methods and encourages us to re-think ways to connect people with organizational performance.

'Hmm' responded Rachel. 'You know, most if not all of the points seem to be the right things to do but the question remains, how to do this in an effective way? I mean, are you suggesting that these are one-size solution for all? Pabloo quickly realized the depth of the quality questions coming from Rachel. To a large extent, it showcased her HR work experience. 'I am glad that you asked that question Rachel' mentioned Pabloo.

Though all these are time tested, in my personal opinion what works in one organization does not necessarily work with another one. You need to figure out as an HR leader what works for you in your organization'. 'I agree!' said Michael, 'even as a teacher I practice that style. Every student has a preferred way of learning.' 'Precisely!' said Pabloo, 'on the same lines in a larger context, what works in Budapest need not necessarily work in Bangalore but to a large extent many of the initiatives will fall under this broad umbrella of seven components – The Human Equation.'

And amidst the serious conversation, it started drizzling. 'Ohh no!' said Pabloo feeling the cold evening and said 'It is starting to rain!'. 'It is quite common in this season of the year' mentioned Michael. 'It won't be much of a bother as it will only drizzle for some time.' Just as he was completing the sentence, there was thunder and it started to rain. 'Well, so much for my prediction' uttered Michael and the three started to quickly walk towards a shelter. As they walked briskly, Pabloo quickly caught a glimpse of the river Danube on the other side, it was looking beautiful. Walking a few steps they spotted a small shelter nearby but the three of them by then were fully drenched in the rain. Pabloo with chattering teeth asked Michael and Rachel 'so what to do?'

'Ice Cream!' screamed Rachel looking at a mobile ice cream seller near them.

Mid-Night Ice Cream and Rains

'Ice Cream in the rains...well, why not??' said Pabloo trying to control his teeth chattering. Rachel could not help laughing at Pabloo. Michael said, 'Rachel has this strange habit of eating ice creams in the rain. Are you up to it?'. 'Millennials...They are different!' thought Pabloo and answered 'I am game! After all, I am on a different continent; I'm allowed to break some rules'. They called out the ice cream seller; he made a nice scoop for the three of them as they sat in the shelter. It was a different experience for Pabloo and he totally enjoyed it.

After all, it is Pabloo, something new and exciting always brings energy to him. 'So, what are your suggestions for an effective HR strategy?' asked Rachel looking at Pabloo. 'Well, as I mentioned earlier, HR can contribute to various factors. An eclectic approach would suit the purpose. To begin with, they can strategize to build the right organizational culture.' said Pabloo.

'You mean like a national culture' asked Michael. 'Precisely, like a national culture, there is a specific culture in each organization and to some extent, national and institutional factors also play a key role in shaping this. Importantly, it is up to the people at the leadership level to set the organizational culture and HR has a job of building it for sustainable organizational performance' replied Pabloo. 'But is not culture in itself a broad term? I mean, I can understand if different organizations in different countries have cultural differences. But I just can't make out how different organizations in the same country, or in that case in the same city can have different cultures.' asked Micheal.

Pabloo acknowledged Michael's question and said 'I understand your question. You see, according to the cultural guru Edgar Schein, organizational culture[26] is a pattern of shared basic assumptions that the group learned that have worked well enough to be considered valid and therefore, to be taught to new members as the correct way to perceive, think, and feel. A more informal definition of culture is the way we do things around here. Some of the organizational cultures that I can quote as examples are: - Work hard – Play hard, Tough Macho Culture, Bet the company culture, etc.'

Michael was amazed and interested to know the details 'wow, sounds interesting! So what are the differences between these cultures and how is culture linked to strategy?' 'Those are really good questions Michael' replied Pabloo. 'Let me first explain how culture is linked to an effective strategy outcome before letting you know about the difference between different organizational cultures. The famous Peter Drucker once said culture can eat your strategy for breakfast![27] It can be true because of a simple reason, culture is your belief system that is lived and experienced by your people, in other words, it is present, and strategy is more futuristic. You cannot win your strategy over culture because people will be more loyal to the culture than the strategy. There are a thousand case studies on both of these, and it every time proves, culture gets a better hand'. 'I agree!' mentioned Rachel nodding her head 'and 'that is why change is such a difficult part of the strategy'.

'Well said Rachel!' lauded Pabloo. 'You see, any change generally startles people given the experience of its prevailing organizational culture and it is usually expressed in the form of resistance to change and in turn, it affects the progress of any strategy'. Michael just thought through for a second or two and stated 'Are you suggesting that change is resisted? As

---

[26] Schein, E (2010) Organizational Culture and Leadership (The Jossey–Bass Business & Management Series), John Wiley & Sons.

[27] Edgar, D., & Stonehouse, G., (2011), Business Strategy: An Introduction, Third Edition, Quote Page 263, Palgrave Macmillan, London.

humans, we have evolved all through the centuries because we adapted to change. We all know the survival of the fittest theory by Charles Darwin and how he put forward his argument that the biological species that survive most effectively are not those which are strongest or most intelligent, but those which are best at adapting to change'.

Pabloo quickly responded to Michael 'I think I need to clarify something here, I did not mean to say people do not change, I meant to say, generally, there may, and in most cases, will be a resistance to change given the cultural context. On the other side, we also have a lot of successful organizations embedding change as part of their culture as well'. Rachel challenged his viewpoints from a different perspective asking 'And why is change important Pabloo, I mean we all understand if the company is not doing well it warrants a change but when everything looks well placed for the company, why should we risk it and change anything in the first place?' Pabloo added, 'Well, I'm not suggesting that you should keep changing things irrespective of the results, I'm saying, you should prepare your culture to embrace change. This applies to organizations that are successful also. Let me put it this way, most of the organizations that started a decade or so are successful today and are not the same as how they started 10 years before. It gives you a simple correlation organization embracing change tends to be more successful, just like the Charles Darwin theory. And that is why building the right culture is such an important aspect of strategy'. 'Good point! I liked the correlation part' added Rachel. Pabloo smilingly clarified, 'Honestly, none of these are my inputs Rachel; these are all insights by some successful HR scholars and leaders of past and present. I just do my part correlating with my limited HR experience.'

Michael respected his honesty. As a Principal of an educational institution, Michael emphasis a lot on value systems and he was happy to meet and strike up a conversation with someone with good values. Just quickly coming back to the conversation, Michael asked, 'so how do we build or change to a culture which embraces change and before you answer that, I'm curious to know about the different organizational cultures, work hard-earn hard?'. 'It is Work hard-Play hard dad' quipped Rachel. 'That is correct!' mentioned Pabloo. 'You see, two brilliant minds, Deal and Kennedy, put forward four different types of culture that prevail in any organization[28]. They differentiated it based on two market factors namely, feedback speed and degree of risk. The four different types of cultures are: - Work hard – Play hard, Tough Macho, Bet your company and Process culture.

In 'Work hard-play hard' organizations, the energy levels are high and the workforce is generally upbeat. Employees themselves take few risks; however, the feedback on how well they are performing is almost immediate. Such cultures prevail in sales organizations. In a 'Touch Macho' culture organization, on the other hand, employees enjoy taking high risks and get feedback almost immediately. Such cultures are common among advertising, sports and entertainment organizations. In a 'Bet your company's culture, the decisions making process involves high risk but the feedback system is slow, pharmaceutical companies are examples of such cultures. Lastly, it is the 'Process cultured' organizations where the feedback and risk are slow and low, examples of such organizations are bank firms and government organizations.'

'Hold on a second there please, I have a question here' asked Michael. 'Are you saying that process culture is bad?' Pabloo looked at him and said, 'there is no such thing as a good or bad culture within this framework, Michael. it is about what is appropriate for the organization for sustainable performance and development.' Michael stood blank hearing the clarification. 'To quote an example, you cannot have a culture which is high in risk such as Touch Macho culture in government organizations because of ultra vires', mentioned Pabloo. 'Ultra vires? Do you mean some sort of epidemic disease?' quipped Michael. *Dad, if an act requires legal authority and it is done with such authority; it is characterized in law as intra vires («within the powers»). If it is done without such authority, it is ultra vires'* Rachel explained this to her

---

[28]   Deal, T. and Kennedy, A. (1982) Corporate Cultures, Basic Books.

dad. 'That is correct Rachel, you see Michael, unlike the private sector, which can do anything other than what the law specifically forbids, Public organizations can only do what the law permits and recommends them. This means that public officials require legal authority for all actions they perform. This means they have to follow lengthy processes and procedures and simply cannot afford to take any risks'. 'I get the drift' mentioned Michael, 'well, this brings me to the next question, how do we change or build a culture?' Just then, the alarm beeped and it was midnight and Pabloo also realized the rain had abated, but he did not bother as the conversation was getting interesting in a way that he was eager to say and Michael and Rachel were all ears.

'Changing or building a culture is not an overnight activity, it takes years to build one, and as I mentioned earlier, the key here would be to build or change the culture for the overall development and sustainable performance of the organization. There are many approaches to it. If I have to pick one, then it would be AI', mentioned Pabloo. 'AI, you mean Artificial Intelligence? So, are you suggesting that we replace people with robots' asked Michael with excitement and curiosity.

Pabloo mentioned, 'I'm suggesting changing people into real people', he quickly sprang further before Michael asked him another question 'AI stands for Appreciative Inquiry[29]. Before he could add anything further, this time Rachel's phone beeped, she quickly excused herself for a minute, returned back and said 'Dad, mom is worried about you'. 'Ohh am surprised!' joked Michael and the three of them shared laughter. Pabloo also mentioned, 'perhaps, it is just about the time I also return to the hotel'. 'Fair but only if we agree on a time when are we catching up tomorrow' mentioned Michael. 'We can catch up a little early tomorrow if you guys are good with it', mentioned Pabloo. 'You see, tomorrow is a light day for us and the guided tour gets over by lunch'. 'Deal!' said Michael 'and this time, I would like to choose a place

---

[29] Srivatsva, S., Cooperrider, D., (1999) Appreciative Management and Leadership, The power of positive Thought and Action in Organizations, Williams Custom.

where we pick up our conversation'. 'Sure, and where would this be?' asked Pabloo. 'That is a surprise', mentioned Michael. 'We will pick you up by 2 PM from this same spot!' With this the three of them bid good night and parted ways. As Pabloo walked back, he was having the same feeling of contentment as last night, only this time it was more filling.

<h1 style="text-align:center">The Third Afternoon</h1>

The third day in Budapest, Hungary, was a very different experience for Pabloo as it was a city tour. He, along with the team visited the Thermal baths. Pabloo enjoyed a hot dip bath which was indeed a soothing and a refreshing experience. On their drive back to the hotel, they stopped at an Indian restaurant for an early lunch. It was a good decision to do that as the entire team had their appetite worked up, thanks to the bath. The effect was also on Pabloo, who otherwise prefers to have his lunch in one sitting. As he fixed himself for a delicious second sitting, the CEO was next in line to him.

'Enjoying the Indian food Pabloo, there is nothing like home food eh?' Singh quipped.

'Yeah, and the food is yummy', responded Pabloo.

'Join me Pabloo', Singh said as he walked towards a two-seater table. 'So, how is it going? Are you planning to do some shopping in the afternoon?'

'No chief, I have other plans', mentioned Pabloo and shared his last two day's evening experience.

'Wow!' smiled Singh and said 'So you never cease to impress people about HR?'

'As much as little it is, I guess I do my part. For me, HR is still underrated, and I want to contribute in some way to make it big'. And while saying this, he noticed Singh was taking his usual judging posture, so he quickly further added, 'this statement about HR that I made has nothing to do with our organization, so don't fire me yet', and they both laughed out loud.

Singh likes Pabloo, though Pabloo is just 38 years old, he often demonstrates the traits and qualities of a highly experienced leader. Among all the qualities of Pabloo, Singh totally admires his enthusiasm and determination to do things!

'No, seriously Pabloo, why would you feel HR is underrated? I mean, I am able to see the difference in the last 10 years or so.'

It was a valuable comment made by the CEO. Singh has 3 decades of work experience and has worked in blue-chip companies at the leadership level before starting this venture.

'I agree chief. But still, HR's potential is not realized by many companies, it is still viewed as a support department.'

'Well Yes, I agree with that. Makes you wonder why it is that way?'

'Maybe it is because HR as a function within organizations is infinitely flexible, organizationally contingent over time and driven principally by the external context of the age: and these often change within a shorter period. The history of HR all over shows it has had to change its priorities and focus its activities by re-inventing itself continuously as a response to external socio-economic factors beyond the immediate control of HR practitioners or senior managers.'

Singh appreciated the depth of the comment, 'well said Pabloo!'

Pabloo looked at him and said 'It is not my comment chief, I read about it in a preparatory CIPD (charter institute of personal development) book'.[10]

'Still Pabloo, I appreciate the fact that you are using it practically'.

---

[10]   Farnham, D., (2015) Human Resource Management in Context, Kogan Page.

The admiration Singh had for Pabloo is mutual as Pabloo always felt Singh is a fantastic coach and mentor. He is successful as CEO simply because of his unique working style. He values every single person's view and appreciates his employees for their strengths.

'So Pabloo, let me ask you a question, what do you think should be done if we have to make organizations realize their HR department's fullest potential?'

'Maybe organizations should not have an HR department in their roles', mentioned Pabloo with his eyes sparkling.

Singh was looking very plain and was clueless about the comment, 'hold on Pabloo, so you are trying to say that we should not have an HR department?'

'No chief, we should have an HR department but it should not be in the organization's payroll. Maybe they should be an individual body nominating HR department for each organization. If not, the entire department at least the HR head' mentioned Pabloo.

'Well, I would love to talk about this' mentioned Singh, 'not as a CEO but as someone from a neutral standpoint. I tell you what, you are aware that we are going to Bratislava, Slovakia early morning. It is just over a two-hour road trip, we should talk about it during our journey. By the way, where did you borrow this idea from?' asked Singh jokingly.

'This chief is my own idea!'

As they walked back to their hotel Singh was thinking about Pablo, 'a real HR leader in the making!' he told himself. He was confident that one-day Pabloo will make a real difference to HR.

Around a quarter to 2 PM, Pabloo was all dressed up and made his way to the agreed spot. As he came close by, he noticed a bright red sedan.

'Hop in Pabloo, we are going for a ride.'

Pabloo got in and tied the seat belt, 'Rachel has sent her apologies. She is caught up with an office meeting but will join us in the evening and she has also cautioned me not to discuss AI until she joins us' mentioned Michael.

Pabloo smiled and asked, 'where are we headed?'

'You will see.'

It was a swift 20 minutes ride inside one of the most beautiful cities Pabloo has seen. Pabloo was silently observing Michael's style of driving. He was much disciplined in following the rules. Just for a second, he allowed his HR mind to judge this man. Michael came across as someone very responsible in his actions and thoughts. His curiosity and willingness to understand and respect the perspective of others seem to be his key strength. Michael seems to be apt in his role as a teacher and a principal. The car turned sharply to one of those medieval-looking buildings. Another museum or a castle in store thought Pabloo, not that he did not enjoy any of those but he hoped it would be something a little more exciting. They parked the car and walked straight into the building. Pabloo noticed a series of signage boards in the local language leading to the building. There was a tennis and basketball court on the other side of the building with some enthusiastic participants. Where are we? wondered Pabloo. By the time they reached the building and climbed up the stairs, he noticed people wishing Michael in the local dialect. They then took a quick sharp turn towards a long corridor and even before Pabloo could think further, Michael opened a door onto his left side for Pabloo and mentioned, 'Welcome to our college!'

Pabloo was amazed and super excited. As they walked further, he noticed the door leading to a small auditorium. Facing him, he saw close to 25 to 30 students on the other side. They all looked in their early 20s and were quite busy speaking to each other until about the time Michael was visible on the platform. The absolute buzz dropped to a pin-drop silence in a matter of seconds. Michael walking alongside Pabloo made their way to the nicely arranged seats on the platform facing the students. Michael offered a seat to Pabloo and made his way to the presenter mike. As Pabloo sat, he remembered his old college days.

'My dear bright minds,' quipped Michael in English, 'thanks for accepting my invitation to assemble in the auditorium on such short notice. On behalf of everyone here, I would like to extend a very warm welcome to Pabloo to our college'. A loud applause followed the welcome. It was a long one and Pabloo stood up in respect, it was a great experience for him. 'Students...' continued Michael, 'I would like to point out that I got to know Pabloo in the last 48 hours before which he was a stranger to me.

He is a successful Human Resource professional heading a small corporation hailing from Bangalore, India. He has come here for a business celebration visit. I bumped into him quite accidentally but clearly, it was one of the best meets that I have had with a stranger. I strongly believe he will make a difference to every single final-year student here who is poised to become the future leaders of our country and our economy'.

He looked at Pabloo and mentioned, 'Pabloo, I know you were not prepared for this meet. But I request you to spend and share some of your People management experience with these bright young minds. All of these students understand English fluently and I'm confident that you will make a difference to them!' Pabloo's eyes lit up hearing the magical word 'difference'.

Michael looked back at the students for a brief second and mentioned, 'Boys and Girls, welcome Pabloo to the stage'. Applause followed and Pabloo walked toward the mike. He was a frequent visitor to college campuses back in Bangalore as a campus recruiter and enjoyed conversing with students. Although this was a different experience, his enthusiasm and energy pumped up, he was determined to make a difference!

The Millennials

'Greetings Hungary', echoed Pabloo's voice 'Well, I was not expecting this' he mentioned smilingly 'but glad, I'm here now, I have not prepared any presentation or speech formally but I would love to interact with you all. Maybe, all of us should treat this as a freewheeling session and make it worthwhile. To begin with, I'm curious to know what questions you have for me', mentioned Pabloo.

After about 15 seconds of silence, one student stood up and asked, 'How do you like our country?'

'It's beautiful!' said Pabloo almost immediately. 'I am not a frequent traveler to other countries, but with my limited visits to close to 10 countries, so far, Hungary is the best!' A loud cheering followed, Pabloo also noticed the students were warming up and some possible serious questions were on his way.

Just by then, another student stood up and said 'Hi, my name is Hanna. I am a final-year student majoring in Economics. I know to a large extent that HR is linked with economics. Therefore, I want to know your viewpoints about Globalization?'

Pabloo was quiet thinking about something for a second or two and asked, 'Hanna, can you be a little specific?'

'Sure, you see, some people believe that globalization would eventually wipe out the natural resources much to the harm of humankind and there is another set of people who feel globalization is much needed for the prosperity of nations and the global economy. What are your viewpoints and how do you think students like us should respond to this?'

'Such a profound question Hanna. Well, I will try my best to answer it. You see, globalization has always been a controversial subject. Broadly, it would be the internationalization of economic activity as well as its social, cultural, and political dimensions. The essence of globalization is that national economies become networked with other economies worldwide through international trading, information and computer technologies, and common consumerism driven by sophisticated marketing techniques. As rightly mentioned, there are two schools of thought about globalization. Its proponents argue globalization increases employment opportunities, increases free trade and creates common platforms and groups to fight terrorism, climate change, etc. Skeptics of globalization on the other hand point out market failure, market creep namely one person – one dollar, and environmental concerns, etc.[11] Truly, there is a big concern about the depletion of natural resources. From the viewpoint of young people's minds, the key concern is that it brings in widening division among people as much as it brings people together, and race to the bottom.

---

[11] Farnham, D., (2015) Human Resource Management in Context, Kogan Page.

'Greetings Hungary'

Hanna interrupted, 'How something that brings people together can divide people?

'Inequality! You see in one of the UN meetings, it was presented that the assets of the 200 richest people on earth are greater than the combined incomes of more than 2 billion of the poorest, and the gap between the two groups continues to grow[12]. The US, Europe and Japan are now 100 times richer on average than Ethiopia, Haiti and Nepal, basically because the former has been growing for the last 100 years and the latter has not. That difference across countries was about 9 to 1 at the dawn of the 20th century. Rapid growth in India and China, two of the world›s biggest upcoming economies, means inequality across the world›s people is beginning to decline. But the decline is from astonishingly high levels. Differences in personal income (comparing the richest

---

[12] Wolf, M., (2000) Stepping Stone from Poverty and the big lie of global inequality, Financial Times.

10 percent of Americans to the poorest 10 percent of Ethiopians for example) are well above 10,000 to 1, not 100 to 1[13]. Globalization plays its part in this inequality for a simple reason; the tremendous economic gains associated with deeper and more efficient global markets are not equally shared. Markets, after all, reward those who have the right assets – financial capital, human capital, and entrepreneurial skills. Simply put the rich get richer and the poor get poorer!

'I get it!' mentioned Hanna. Someone from the side asked, 'what is the race to the bottom then?' Pabloo turned to his side to acknowledge the familiar voice. You cannot have Michael without asking questions, he thought. 'You see Michael, Race to the bottom is a popular phrase that states all development happens at the expense of the environment. Larger corporations and MNCs may arrange to be exempted from the local laws about the environment or simply move to a country where the law is not enforced. All these result in increased pollution and greenhouse emission. Natural resources are consumed and depleted leaving nothing for the future generation. Michael nodded agreeing to Pabloo's explanation. Hanna asked, 'So then globalization is not a good thing and we should stop it then?' Pabloo looked straight at her and mentioned 'Globalization is not a bad thing also; It will be foolish to dismiss it that way. We all know the benefits of it improving the overall prosperity of economies. In my opinion, we should approach it responsibly. 'You mean, join the green peace or something?' asked Hanna. 'No, I did not mean it that way, Hanna. Joining a pressure group alone is not the answer; I am saying a responsible way in our choices and decisions is much needed. In other words, being a responsible citizen. Every single person in this room will be contributing to both the country as well as the global economy through your job role. We just need to be cognizant of the fact that our choices and decisions will impact at some level the overall outcome in both inequality and race to the bottom.

---

[13] Birdall,N., (2005). Rising Inequility in the New Global Economy, University of California, Berkley, World Institute for Development Economics Research.

So the key here is to be 'aware' at an individual level. This awareness can only be created if you approach it responsibly. There are many ways to increase awareness importantly it starts within you. Increasing Emotional intelligence is a powerful way to increase awareness of self and social aspects. Once done, there are many ways you can contribute to reducing the ill effects of globalization. To begin with, from this moment on, you can contribute by avoiding any discrimination and having an overall inclusive approach. When harnessed with a large interest in the well-being of everyone and our planet, our thoughts and actions will translate into the right decisions and choices that will benefit not just the nation but the entire world. And as youngsters, you can make a strong influence by setting precedence for not just your generation but for the future as well'. He noticed a lot of youngsters on the other side nodded in acknowledgment.

Another student stood up and introduced himself as Tommy 'I have a question; I want to get your views related to skill sets and qualifications. The world seems to be moving at a fast pace, the skills that you have acquired in the past are becoming redundant. Therefore how should we approach the future?'

'Well Tommy, you are bang on about the pace and the redundancy, a suitable term for that would be Disruptive Innovation'. Noticing the silence, Pabloo further added, 'Disruptive innovation by definition refers to an innovation that creates a new market and value network and eventually disrupts an existing market and value network, displacing established market leading firms, products, and alliances[14]. A classic example of how disruptive innovation can throw established businesses out of context would be film-based model of digital photography, a much more recent example would be cell phones to smartphones. All these are examples of how things can change quickly and how it is important for us to constantly upgrade our skills. So, if

------

[14] Bower, J. and Christensen, C., (1995), Disruptive Technologies: Catching the wave, Harvard Business School Pub.

your question is how you should be prepared for the future, then my answer to you is to keep updating your knowledge and skills. If you are wondering how to do it effectively, then my answer is to know your strength and interest and keep building on them. If you want a tip, then I would suggest 70:20:10, blended learning towards your interest[15]. It states 70% of learning is experiential. It happens through daily tasks, challenges and practice. 20% of learning is social. It happens through learning, coaching, mentoring and collaborative learning. The last 10% of learning is formal and It happens through structured training courses and programs. One way of making this a reality for you would be to engage in out-of-school programs classes such as common group forums, workshops, interns, etc. Please remember, you cannot stop progress but you can always prepare yourself to handle it well.'

Pabloo noticed the students nodding in agreement with the point made. Just as he thought that there were no further questions, three more hands were raised!

---

[15] Jennings, C., (2013), 70:20:10 Framework Explained, Creating High Performance Cultures, Forum Pty Limited.

Questions Galore

'My name is Emma and I am 22 years old. I keep hearing this Gen Y, Gen X, etc. What is it all about and why is this differentiated or classified that way? I mean, what are the purpose and the benefit?'.

'A generation is all of the people born and living at about the same time, regarded collectively. Currently, on this planet, humans are from five generations[16]. They are Gen Z, iGen, or Centennials: Born in 1996 and later. Millennials or Gen Y: 1977 to 1995 born. Generation X: 1965 to 1976 born. Baby Boomers: 1946 to 1964 born. Lastly, Traditionalists or Silent Generation: Born in 1945 and before. Although there is a little disagreement on the precise years, broadly these are commonly accepted across the globe. Now, this classification of generations has become an interesting topic from a market standpoint or for that case, the workplace. Studies have shown each of these generations exhibits certain unique characteristics and traits. Simply put from a workplace standpoint, certain preferences over others. To quote an example, Gen X is found to be more loyal to their employers when compared to Gen Y. Another example is Generation Y places Brand and Autonomy as the highest drivers for them in a workplace than any other generation. If we go by statistics, then Gen Y and Z is poised to be over 50% of

---

[16] Strauss, W. and Howe, N., (1997), The Fourth Turning, What the cycles of History Tell Us About America's Next Rendezvous with Destiny, Crown.

the global workforce by 2025'. Pabloo paused for a second and said smilingly 'That is you guys here!'[17].

To answer your question explicitly considering the benefit standpoint from a workplace, it helps to drive higher engagement. Now, if I want to offer all of you guys jobs in my company, I will only do justice if I can create the right environment that motivates you for higher performance, in other words, a great engagement. Gen Y prefers Innovation in workplace, if that is the case, bureaucracy has to be killed!'

Emma looked occupied in her mind and asked 'If that is the case, won't all organizations be the same then in creating an innovative environment for Gen Y?

'Well, for one thing, the world seems to be moving towards it' mentioned Pabloo. *'At the same time, we need to understand that not everything that fits molds. What I mean is a lot of variables also play along. To quote an example,* there may be differences between a country because of national and institutional factors. But to a large extent, the classification of generations benefits the workplace'

The next question comes from a girl, 'Hi, I'm Brenda. I am pursuing my final year master's in Finance. I have a career ambition of joining a Fortune 100 company and making it to a leadership role. I would like to hear your viewpoints on women empowerment. The reason that I'm asking you this question is that I read an article that claimed that there are lesser women in leadership roles'.

'Brenda, there has never been a better time for women to have greater career ambitions' mentioned Pabloo almost instantaneously. 'The failure of women to make progress into leadership positions is usually referred to by the metaphor of a 'glass ceiling'. But the good news is that it is changing fast. I say this because most companies have realized the

---

[17]   Harjani, A., (2014), From brats to bosses – Gen Y to dominated by 2025. https://www.cnbc.com/2014/01/22/to-bosses--gen-y-to-dominate-by-2025.html.

value of women at all levels, importantly in leadership. You will also be happy to know that the traditional, deeply rooted patriarchal mindset is changing in many organizations. Yes, the world is waking up, more than ever, to the power of women in the global workforce. But at the same time, they also realize there is still a long way to go. To propel this, many companies have diversity and inclusion strategies such as 20/20 targets, i.e., increasing the percentage of women leadership by 20% at the board level. European Commission released an article[18] recently on International Women's Day and mentioned that the world of work is on track to meet the target of 40% female representation in middle and senior management positions. And Brenda, if your ambition is to get into the fortune 100 companies, then you will be interested in the 30% club. It was started in the year 2010 originally in the UK but has its chapters in many countries including the United States. It campaigns for greater representation of women on the FTSE100 boards with a target of a minimum of 30%. As I said earlier, it is an exciting time for women pursuing careers in leadership.' concluded Pabloo.

'Hi, Pabloo! My name is Dora and I am pursuing my final year in Business administration. I wanted to get into academia. I wanted to know how this contributes to the country's economy. In a much simpler way, how can education contribute in a better way to the country's economy?'

'It is well established that improvements in education are associated with long-term improvements in economic performance. The success of the developed economic countries and the developing tiger economic countries with their growing educational levels are the standing examples of this. There are various reasons for it with the primary being an educational qualification being a pre-requisite for the workforce. In general, education and economic performance are likely to be interlinked for a simple reason, that is having a more

---

[18] European Commission, (2002), Commission welcomes political agreement on Gender Balance on Corporate Boards. https://ec.europa.eu/commission/presscorner/detail/en/IP_22_3478.

educated workforce enables firms to take advantage of new economic opportunities, leading to improved performance. Also, economic growth can lead to greater national and personal wealth, which increases the resources available and education opportunities. Broadly, there are three theories linking education and economic growth. The first one is the basic human capital approach, which states education improves the overall skills and abilities of the workforce, leading to greater productivity and improved ability to use existing technology, thus contributing to economic growth. The second, the innovation approach links education to improving the capacity of the economy to develop new ideas and technologies. And the third extension of this is the knowledge transfer approach, which sees education as a means of spreading the knowledge needed to apply new ideas and make use of new technologies. So Dora, suppose you get into research, the rationale is that your research outcome will contribute to, let's say technology or innovation and that in turn will link up to improved performance and eventually to the growth of the economy. That is how the process connects and unfolds.

'My name is Jim and I am pursuing management. I wanted to be a successful entrepreneur. How do I become a Jack Ma or Jeff Bezos? Importantly, how do I not become part of the list of spectacularly unsuccessful leaders who wanted to become Jack Ma or Jeff Bezos? Do I just need to be just lucky?

Pabloo retorted 'Jim, both successful and unsuccessful entrepreneurs almost share the same traits. And yes, we cannot discount the luck factor! As we speak about luck, I am reminded of a Roman philosopher, Seneca who said, Luck happens when Preparation meets Opportunity! I think this is one of the most important key factors that contribute to success! So if you want to be a successful entrepreneur, start the preparation and at one time or the other, the opportunity will present itself. At this juncture of your life, persistence would be an important preparation. Eventually, when you hit the market, the ability to influence others will be another key factor. Another differentiating factor would be to recognize the opportunity and take the risk. There is almost a positive connotation between entrepreneurs and their willingness to take risks.

It would help if you also remembered that Jack Ma or Jeff Bezos are not strangers to failures. Most successful entrepreneurs reach their peak only after multiple failures. You need to realize that your grit determines your success, ensuring that your idea, product, or service differentiates itself with value. Suppose it is a product-based endeavor; you must mesh innovation in all your business strategies. Innovation is the vehicle for a successful entrepreneur; the entrepreneur systematically looks for change, responds to them, and takes advantage of opportunities as they present themselves.

There was research conducted through psychological testing of 4,000 successful entrepreneurs from several countries against 1,800 business leaders who described themselves as general managers but not entrepreneurs. The results revealed that the two groups had 28 of 41 dimensions of leadership in common. But further analysis revealed that entrepreneurs had three main unique characteristics: the ability to thrive in uncertainty, a passionate desire to author and own projects, and unique skill at persuasion[19]. *In India, we have a saying, "If you are destined to be, you will!"* So Jim, in other words, it is the right time that you should start writing your destiny!

'Hi Pabloo, I'm Sara. I have a sort of personal question. This is about me, I never thought I would openly talk about this but your answers to the questions are insightful and hence I'm mustering the courage. Sometimes I feel less about myself in a group discussion. In my self-assessment in such situations, many of the members of the group can express themselves confidently though their knowledge on that subject is limited. On the other hand, I'm not entirely confident in speaking in-depth though my understanding of the subject is high or at least

---

[19] Butler,T.,"Hiring an Entrepreneurial Leader: What to Look For." Harvard Business Review 95, no. 2 (March–April 2017): 85–93.

better than most others in the group. Lately, it is bothering me a lot and making me feel low and depressed.'

Pabloo paused for a few seconds and mentioned 'It seems to be a classic instance of Dunning- Kruger effect"[20]. Dunning and Kruger, two brilliant social psychologists, pointed to a cognitive bias that most people are subjected to. They proved through their research that people with less competence tend to rate themselves high and on the other hand those with higher competence underestimate themselves. This in turn impacts their belief and behavior. A simple example of it is if we give a piece of paper to all the students in this auditorium and ask them to rate themselves on a scale of 10. Most often the students will either over-rate or under-rate themselves. An actual comparison with a neutral performance evaluation will show the flawed ratings. In your case as well, you may underrate yourself. In my own thinking Sara, the cause of your feeling is primarily because of comparison. If anything Sara, take heart from the famous saying "Empty vessels make more noise". Therefore, do not provide any opportunity for self-doubt in such situations. If anything, you should increase your awareness and the best way to deal with it is to measure your progress from what you were yesterday to where you are today! Simply work on your Range. I usually employ my very own RANGE technique for self-improvement and awareness'.

Range in its most essential meaning, in simple mathematical terms, would be 'the difference between the lowest and highest values'. In {4, 6, 9, 3, 7} the lowest value is 3, and the highest is 9, so the range is 9 – 3 = 6. Our objective should be to keep the range maximum and if you understand this correctly Sara then you will realize it is not about

---

[20] Kruger, J., & Dunning, D. (1999). Unskilled and unaware of it: How difficulties in recognizing one's own incompetence lead to inflated self-assessments. Journal of Personality and Social Psychology, 77(6), 1121–1134. https://doi. org/10.1037/0022-3514.77.6.1121.

ranking and it does not matter where you are now, what truly matters is where we will be!

Simply put, the journey from our low points to peak performance on what we consider important to us. The technique of RANGE is the acronym of:

- R - Reflection and Reinforcement
- A - Awareness and Action
- N - Never compare with others but yourself
- G - Get support from others and become better
- E - Express and Enjoy yourself

'Agree' mentioned Sara. 'I will start to work on my range!'

'Great' smiled Pabloo.

'All right Students let us take that one last question.' Michael mentioned aloud from his seat.

'Hi Pabloo, This is James and I am from Malaysia. I have come down to this University to pursue my Masters. The decision to take an overseas education was not an easy one. In this world of the web, multiple e-learning platforms make it easier for one to access quality education. My question is if the full-time university education is losing its value. Even with or without it, is e-learning as effective as it is projected?'

Michael also looked absorbed in the question and was excited to hear Pabloo. Pabloo mentioned 'Honestly I do not know if the full-time courses at universities are losing value. We will have to wait and see how the education space turns out. But I can try and attempt if e-learning is an effective platform. E-learning scores are very high for being a learning platform anytime and anywhere! But at the same time, e-learning platforms are also evolving now. It scores less when compared to classroom learning which allows more dialogues, questions and group discussions, etc. That being said, colossal information is available on the world web about any subject. I think it comes to the learner on the choice and preference. What we need to take into consideration is the learning style of people. Everyone has their preference of choice when it comes to learning. Studies are showing the preference of the younger generation is inclined toward the online platform. Eventually, with Gen Y and Gen Z taking over as the largest working population, there definitely will be more focus on e-learning. Already there is a lot of progress through gamification as a way of creating interest in learning. In my own opinion, perhaps e-learning is very powerful when it is blended with other methods.

'Thank you Pabloo' said Michael and added 'James, let me assure you, a full-time education will never lose its value. It prepares you as a well-rounded individual to take on the challenges of the real world. As Pabloo mentioned, eventually a hybrid model may be the way. But the greatest value will always be driven by a full-time education.'

After addressing James, Michael was just about to walk towards the Mic when another student stood up and said, 'Hold on Michael, I have one last question for Pabloo' and she continued 'I am Zoe! Perusing masters in Psychology. I found all your answers informative. If I have to ask you, what are the two important qualities through which we can differentiate ourselves, what will be your answer and how do we do it?'

Pabloo's eyes again lit up; after all, it is about the magical word 'Difference!' The students also seemed to be looking forward to his last answer. Pabloo was looking straight into the eyes of Zoe and there was a hiatus for almost a minute. Michael broke the silence and said, 'Pabloo, are you with us?'

'I am Michael', mentioned Pabloo still looking at Zoe. 'It's just that I wanted to truly attempt to answer the question to make a difference'. He continued 'Zoe, I might sound a little spiritual but here is my answer. To differentiate yourself, you need to keep your thinking and action different from others. It does not mean irrationality, it means being able to see what others are not able to see and able to do what others are not able to do. One way of doing that is by dividing your world into

External and Internal. External refers to the external world, anything which is outside you. Internal refers to the world within you. From an external standpoint, have the courage to challenge things that you disagree with. This does not mean arrogance but a genuine approach to seeking the right answers and solutions. From the internal aspect, do not worry about failures instead, use them to reflect upon yourself. If you practice both of these in their true spirit, at some level you will become a highly abled individual as you are linking up your external world by questioning rationally and learning things powerfully with your internal world by self-reflection. You will have an enormous amount of positive influence on others, inspiring both them and yourself to achieve greater heights, simply put, making a difference!

Michael was impressed with his answer, 'Thank you Pabloo!' he mentioned and walked to the Mic. Pabloo just went back to his seat. 'Pabloo, I believe I am speaking for the entire team here. You have made such a good positive impact with your thoughtful answers. I strongly believe this session will help these wonderful youngsters in their career planning. Like you say, to put it simply, You Made A Difference! And I'm sure everyone agrees to it', mentioned Michael. Applause followed it, this time it was a huge and long one with loud cheering. Almost all the students walked towards Pabloo to thank him and exchange goodbyes! Pabloo gave attention and wished each one of the students individually as they embarked on the world of work journey.

Welcome Home

Post the session, Michael took Pabloo for a tour inside the college. It was a beautiful campus with greenery all around. It had a wonderful modern library; a combination of paperback books and digital versions. There was a huge canteen and football play area along with tennis and basketball courts. Michael spoke about his institution with a lot of pride and mentioned specific details about the diverse students and professors. It was an evening to remember for Pabloo with so many youngsters around. Around 6 PM, they both got into the car.

'Now, where are we headed to?' asked curious Pabloo.

'Home, I want to welcome you to my home for dinner. I hope you will like our preparations.'

'Thank you, Michael. I will love it and can't wait to taste it.'

As the car started to move, Pabloo thought about Michael, 'Such a warm personality he has'. Pabloo started liking him and he reminded him of his father, whom he lost about 20 years ago.

And just then Michael asked 'Pabloo, I meant to ask you something! Do you think you can have a talk with Rachel about her career? As I mentioned earlier, Rachel wants to make it big in HR, but lately, she has been complaining about the complication of the role. In fact, last month she spoke to me about options to move to other fields. I'm concerned in a way now, especially in the last 3 days after speaking to you. What I am hearing from you about HR is truly inspiring, and I could not sense any reason why would Rachel want to move out of such an exciting profession. Maybe you should spend some time with her and guide her. You see, as a father, I do not want my daughter to make a quick decision about a field and career she loves the most.

Pabloo reassured Michael and said, 'I will speak to her, not in a way to change her decision but invite her for an open and direct conversation about her interest.'

As the car was moving swiftly, Pabloo again went on remembering his father. His father had a positive influence on him; he was hard-working, focused and always encouraged Pabloo to make a difference in his young years. Pabloo reminisced how his father used to take him to a nearby Orphanage to do social service during the weekends. He wrote the code of value system in Pabloo's young mind. No wonder, Pabloo ended up being a Human Resource professional.

After about 20 minutes of driving, the car made a sharp turn from the main road to a residential complex. Just after 2 minutes of driving, Michael parked the car in a garage and mentioned, 'Welcome to my abode.'

As Pabloo walked along with Michael, he saw Rachel at the entrance.

'Welcome Pabloo!' said Rachel.

It was a nice house with a small lawn covered with a white colored wooden fence. It had a cottage look to it entirely.

Pabloo replied 'Thank you, Rachel!'

Rachel looked at Michael and mentioned 'Mom has gone to the nearby shopping complex, she should join us shortly.'

All three of them entered the house. Pabloo noticed neatly arranged sitting lounges and nice wall hangings. As he shifted his eyes from each of the wall hangings, he was pleasantly surprised to see the portrait of Mahatma Gandhi and before he could ask anything, Michael said, 'A great soul, he taught the entire humanity about principles and values.'

Pabloo looked at Michael with admiring eyes and nodded in agreement. Next to Gandhi was a portrait of Nelson Mandela. Pabloo was able to understand Michael even better now. The portraits were a reflection of Michael's personality. Pabloo turned around and noticed another portrait of Michael standing with a gentleman of his age.

'Who is he?' asked Pabloo curiously.

'He is Ernő Rubik, a Hungarian inventor, architect, and professor of architecture. You will know him better for his invention of mechanical puzzles including the Rubik's Cube. While he became famous for inventing the Rubik's Cube and his other puzzles, much of his recent work involved the promotion of science in education. Among his other key initiatives, he aims to engage students in science, mathematics, and problem-solving at a young age.'

'Are you all good for an early dinner?' echoed another voice, and all 3 of them turned back.

Pabloo saw a lady in her mid-forties. She smiled and said 'Welcome to our home, Pabloo. I am sorry I was not available in person when you arrived.'

'Thank you' said Pabloo instantaneously.

She looked at Michael and mentioned 'and you mentioned the guest will be here by 7 PM?'

'Yes! But we came a little early', said Michael looking apologetic. He then looked at Pabloo and mentioned 'Meet my wife, Judit.'

'Please call me Judy' she mentioned and shook hands with Pabloo.

'It's nice meeting you! And thanks for inviting me over for dinner.'

'It is our pleasure! Let me quickly get you a drink, what would you prefer to have? Apple juice?'

'Sure' mentioned Pabloo.

'There is never a dull moment with my wife around' mentioned Michael smiling.

'Would you prefer with or without ice?' Judy asked from the kitchen.

'Without please.'

All of them sat on the couch in the living room as Judy returned with a tray of glasses and offered them all a drink. She also took her seat and asked 'So Pabloo is it your first visit to Budapest?'

'Yes! But I'm already feeling at home.'

She further added 'I am so fascinated by your country. It is embraced with so many cultures there.'

Michael added 'Judy use to teach history and culture at a local school earlier but she took an early retirement.'

'That's great' said Pabloo.

'In fact, I visited your country once about 20 years ago' mentioned Judy. 'I visited the Taj Mahal and I must tell you that is the most beautiful monument ever built in this world.'

'It is! In fact, there are so many other places within India that are a must-visit for everyone. You see India is a country of unity in diversity. India's languages, religions, dance, music, architecture, food, and customs differ from place to place within the country. The culture is so different in each of the states that you can feel like a national foreigner and enjoy it.'

'National foreigner, eh? That sounds interesting' mentioned Michael.

Pabloo laughed a little, 'I just came up with the word. What I meant was, you can enjoy a varied and diverse culture within the country'.

'So what keeps you guys together?' asked Michael.

Pabloo thought for a second and said 'Cricket!'

Michael had the puzzled look on his face. Rachel intervened 'It is a popular game dad!'

'I am aware of the game Rachel, but could not believe that can be the reason.'

Pabloo explained 'Just kidding Michael, we respect each other's customs and culture, and we strongly believe that our unity is our strength'. Michael nodded in agreement.

Judy stood up and welcomed Pabloo to the dining table, 'I hope you have your appetite worked up Pabloo.'

'Wow, the food looks delicious' Pabloo quipped looking at the dinner spread.

Judy smiled and mentioned 'we have some Gulyás soup with Tofu, Paprika Chicken, some Rakott Krumpli which is a layered potato casserole with sausages, eggs and bacon, a little bit of Hungarian risotto which is a bowl of white rice mixed with green peas. Mézes Krémes, Hungarian Honey Cake & Apricot Kolaches - Chirstmas cookie.'

'Thank you!' mentioned Pabloo as he sat, but he was a little hesitant just before the serving.

'All well Pabloo?' asked Judy caringly as she saw his expressions.

'Yes! Yes! Err..., which of these are vegetarian? Pabloo asked slowly.

Michael replied with concern 'are you vegetarian Pabloo? I am sorry, we did not realize it.'

Judy added with concern 'I should have checked earlier, we are so sorry. Now that you told me, I just got reminded about your country and yes there is a huge community that practices vegetarianism from birth.'

'You are right Judy, but then I do not belong to that community. I am just practicing vegetarianism for the last 8 years' mentioned Pabloo.

'That is incredible' mentioned Michael adding 'not even eggs?'

'No Michael, not even eggs'. Michael as curious as ever asked him again 'may we know the reason why'. 'Sure, it was one among many things towards my journey of spiritualism and transformation. I was inspired by my Guruji towards the journey.

'Guruji?'

'Yes Michael, we have many venerated spiritual leaders in India. I came across his foundation through the practice of Yoga.

Judy chirped 'Oh yes, Yoga. An ancient spiritual discipline from India, it is practiced for the well-being of the mind and soul of an individual.

'Well said Judy!' Pabloo continued 'Yoga is essentially a spiritual discipline based on an extremely subtle science that focuses on bringing harmony between mind and body. It is an art and science of healthy living. The word ‹Yoga› is derived from the Sanskrit word ‹Yuj›, meaning ‹to join› or ‹to yoke› or ‹to unite.'

The word 'Yoga' is derived from the Sanskrit word 'Yuj', meaning 'to join' or 'to yoke' or 'to unite.

'Wow! I thought you were more logical and rational in your approach' said Michael.

'I'm Michael' mentioned Pabloo 'But at some level, science and spirituality combine for a higher being and living.'

'So, what's the plan for dinner then Dad?'

'Well, we will order some vegetarian food from a nearby restaurant' mentioned Michael.

'Judy made this dinner for me, and I can't think of having any food other than that. Besides, more than a billion people go to bed hungry each night so it will be a crime to waste food. Judy, can you please serve the vegetarian dishes in this?

'That would be Gulyás soup with Tofu and the Hungarian risotto' mentioned Judy. She started to like Pabloo already.

A People Conversation between a Baby Boomer, Gen X, and Gen Y – Part 1

After a tasty dinner, Pabloo thanked Judy once again. Around 8.30 pm, Michael, Rachel, and Pabloo sat outside the house on a nice seating. As they enjoyed the evening breeze, Michael said 'I enjoyed the way you answered those questions that came from the students' Pabloo. It was very informative even to me. I also just realized something, I'm 58 years old, my daughter is 25 and I take it you are 40?'

'38 actually! Pabloo said with a grin.

'That makes three generations sit together, a baby boomer, Gen X, and Gen Y?.'

'Oh yes, I did not realize that until about now' said Pabloo in agreement. With all excitement, Rachel asked, 'so, now is the time to discuss AI I guess.'

Michael quickly said 'good point Rachel, Pabloo we are waiting to hear the concept of AI.'

Pabloo responded 'as mentioned earlier, AI stands for Appreciative Inquiry, according to Cooperrider, AI considers the 'best in people, their organization and the world around them'. It does not talk about problems; it is very much against failures and problems for considering success![21].

---

[21] Cooperrider, D., Whitney, D., (2005), Appreciative Enquiry – A positive revolution in Change, Berrett-Koehler Publishers.

It has 4 stages or the 4D's.

The first D is Discovery - Conversations about possibilities,

The second D is Dreaming – Ideas and stories for the future and what might be,

The third D is Designing – Asserting the ambitions into plans for the future, and finally,

The fourth D is Delivery – Action planning around specific activities, tasks and processes.'

'Very interesting and how can this be linked to a culture change?' asked Rachel.

'Well, culture is a collective programming of the organization's mind.[22]. We all know how a disengaged culture can kill an organization, suppose you want to change it to a much-needed engaged one, then you can use AI. Through AI you can establish themes such as increased motivation, better communication, etc. Once the theme is expressed then you can establish the four 4D's for the much-needed outcome.'

'I have a question. How can we have an organization which is disengaged? I mean, it is understandable if we have a few among the lot' asked Michael.

Pabloo nodded and mentioned 'you are right Michael, there cannot be an organization that is 100% disengaged, but generally the disengaged workforce is much higher than the engaged workforce and the larger point is such disengaged employees can have a negative influence on the whole culture. Consider this for an example, Gallup through its recent survey has published that 65% of the US workforce is disengaged and worldwide the number for it is at 85%![23] Clearly, it comes out the

---

[22] Hofstede, G., (2001), Culture's Consequences – Comparing Values, Behaviors, Institution and Organizations Across Nations, SAGE Publications.

[23] State of The Global Workplace, (2017), Gallup Press.

percentage of disengaged employees is a higher proportion than the engaged employees and as HR professionals, we have a responsibility to make it much more engaged for the betterment of the organization and the economy overall.'

'I agree, you need to have a much-engaged workforce' mentioned Rachel, 'but can you be specific as to how we can use this AI and drive towards engagement?' she further asked.

Pabloo thought for a while and mentioned, 'the easiest and the simplest way to do this would be through your line managers. You should train your line managers and people in leadership about the concept of AI and make them understand its true benefits. Line managers generally have the largest span in an organization and most of your people-related issues stem from this relationship. Leadership on the other hand sets the culture. Therefore, these two groups can be initially focused, and eventually the whole organization, for a change through AI. For eg: One study states that on average there are 13 criticisms during performance appraisal and 33% of the time it has a negative impact on performance. If this is the case, an AI themes of motivation such as a sense of meaning and purpose; a sense of choice; a sense of competence; and a sense of progress,[24]. can be established and each line manager can be encouraged to engage with the team on these themes through the four stages of 4D's. Since AI considers only the best in people and the world around them, there will be a shift in the way the line managers address and encourage their team members. This, in turn, can tremendously increase motivation as a drive for higher engagement. Similarly, leadership can set precedence. An AI theme of communication can be established at the leadership level, which in turn can increase the trust level within the organization through transparency leading to higher engagement!'

---

[24] Chalofsky, N.,and Krishna, V., (2009), Meaningfulness, commitment and engagement: The intersection of a deeper level of intrinsic motivation, Advances in Developing Human Resources. 11,189-203.

Rachel had a doubt and straightaway asked Pabloo 'All these concepts that you have shared so far definitely sound convincing at a theoretical level but how far are these practical? We both know, as HR professionals, any change management is going to be resisted by people. So, my question to you is how do we convince them?'

Pabloo was looking forward to answering the question; he liked the questions from Rachel as it always had a clear people aspect to it. 'Rachel, first things first, all the concepts that I have shared so far are not just theoretical but also practical. In fact, there are thousands of success stories in different organizations supporting it. Secondly, we do not have to convince anyone, we need to inspire them. Not in the way of empty promises and lip service, but in the way of commitment and determination to make it happen. Importantly, its progress and outcome should be expressed by authentic data. If all of these should happen, then we need to wear a cap of professional HR and exhibit those unique qualities.'

Rachel raised her eyebrows and said with a smile 'unique qualities? I thought we need to apply common sense more than anything.'

Pabloo answered 'I strongly believe that a successful HR role is unique, unlike any other role in an organization. The most challenging part of it is that it deals with the smartest of creations on this planet, and to deal with them, People managers have to be super smart. I am sure you agree to it and it is a lot more than common sense.'

Rachel smiled sheepishly. Michael added, 'so what are those unique qualities?'

Pabloo looked at both of them and explained, 'there has been quite a bit of research on this right from the time of the industrial revolution when there was a need for pre-personal management and personal management[25]. More recently, Ulrich and Brockbank[26]. *identified the HR specialist›s role as Employee Advocate – HR focuses on the immediate need of the employee, a* Human Capital Developer – HR focuses on preparing employees to be successful in the future, a Functional Expert – HR is concerned with HR practices central to HR values, a Strategic Partner – HR has multiple roles including business expert, change agent, strategic HR planner, knowledge manager, and consultant, with a vision of aligning HR systems to achieve organizational vision and mission, and as a leader – HR leads the HR function, collaborating with other management functions. CIPD, Charter Institute of Personal Development put together a 7 Need to know professional competence of exceptional HR.'

'Another seven? Just like the seven components of the Human equation? asked Michael.

'Yes, something like that Michael. The only thing is they arrived at these seven after speaking to a whole bunch of successful HR leaders. They are:

First, HR practitioners need an understanding of their organization's strategy, Its performance goals and drivers, and the sector in which they work. These cover the market factors impacting performance, including demography, customers, competitors, and globalization. They need to know, understand and speak the language of the business they work for and the full range of human resources levers driving organizational performance.

Second, HR practitioners need a broad understanding and technical capability of 10 HR professional areas, with in-depth knowledge in one or two of them.

---

[25] Morris, S., and Snell, S., (2009), The evolution of HR strategy: adaptations in increasing global complexity. The SAGE handbook of human resource management.

[26] Ulrich, D. and Brockbank, W., (2005), The HR value proposition, Boston: Harvard Business School Press.

Third, they need to know or access relevant employment and discrimination law in both their local and international jurisdictions.

Fourth, they need to know the external and internal influences, including political and economic ones, impacting the directions, shape, and performance of their organization and the HR levers that can be applied within them.

Fifth, HR practitioners need to be able to shape and lead change programs and know how to develop organizational strategies and operating plans in response to these forces.

Sixth, they need to know how to determine organizational capability and resourcing levels to support the delivery of HR strategy and plans.

Finally, HR professionals at the highest levels of professional competence need to know 'what external HR thought leaders and benchmark companies are doing in a variety of areas'. They also need to consider how these lessons 'may apply to their own organization', which necessitates developing 'fit-for-purpose human resources solutions and anticipation of need.'

Rachel looked attentive and said 'I agree, but what about the second one on the technical capability of 10 professional areas? What are those areas?'

'The 10 HR professional areas are organizational design, organizational development, resourcing & talent management, learning & talent development, performance & reward, employee engagement, employee relations, service delivery and information, leading and managing the function, insights, strategy, and solutions' listed Pabloo.

'Oh, these are an ocean of HR activities, is it even possible to cover all aspects? I mean with my limited 5 years of experience, what are my chances?'

Pabloo said 'I agree. But you should know It is classified as different bands based on experience level. As an HR professional with over

5 years of experience, you are expected to exhibit certain aspects of the professional areas. To quote relevance, you are not expected to have strategies, insights, and solutions in the current role that you are performing with your 5-year experience; however, you are expected to take the journey of becoming an HR leader!'

'How will I get there? What are the certain qualities and behaviors I need to acquire? Going back to your point of unique qualities, what are those?' Rachel asked enthusiastically.

Pabloo said, 'the beauty of this model is that they were able to pinpoint the behaviors required to get you there! But before we get there, Michael, may I use your telephone to inform the hotel and my folks that I will be delayed? Michael accompanied him to the telephone and Rachel seemed very curious to know the behaviors.

After finishing the call, Pabloo sat back; he noticed Rachel was all ears. 'Well Rachel, the behaviors that are expected at an individual level are: curiosity, decisive thinking, skilled influencing, credibility, collaborative, driver to deliver, courage to challenge, and role model.'

'Wow! These behaviors will get me there?'

'My answer would be a yes! I tried each of these behaviors and I was able to get results. To be honest with you, it will not be an easy overnight transformation and it is also important to note that these behaviors alone will not yield results but the efforts that you put in towards it will definitely get you there'. Rachel looked a little confused; Pabloo quickly added 'I am saying you need to be genuine in bringing this transformation in you in a way that these behaviors are not superficial or a work mask.'

Michael asked, 'Work mask? What is that? Do you mean employees wear a mask?'

'It simply refers to an artificial masking of behaviors from one's true self' explained Pabloo.

Rachel quickly asked 'is that natural? All of us do change according to the situation, why would anything be wrong with such an approach?'

'All I am saying is it should be a change from inside, not as a reaction to your external environment but as a response within you as a true HR professional. Hope that makes sense' explained Pabloo.

'So if my daughter has to be a successful HR then she should work on these behaviors?'

'Of course Michael, these behaviors should go hand in hand with the 10 professional areas we spoke about. In fact, another global body of HR, SHRM - The Society for Human Resource Management, identifies similar behaviors for professional HR practice. The point here is that transformation is the key!'

The next question came from Rachel, 'so, how do we transform?'

Pabloo looked at her and said *'well, the best way that I know would be to ask yourself, why you should transform?'*

Rachel looked puzzled. Pabloo continued, 'yes Rachel, why do you want to transform in the first case?'

'Simply because I wanted to be a successful HR' Rachel replied confidently.

Pabloo further probed 'and why is that important to you?'

'Because being successful is important to me...'

Pabloo smiled looking at her and said 'I ask the same question again, why is being successful important to you?' Rachel smiled and looked up at the sky thinking deeply.

Michael liked Pabloo's approach. He is keeping his word of not influencing her but having an open and direct conversation.

Rachel continued to gaze at the night sky and mentioned 'I just can't figure it out.'

'All right, let me ask you another question, how will you feel, hear or see if you become successful' asked Pabloo.

Rachel thought and said 'I will feel happy and there will be a sense of achievement in me, there will be a good respect that I will command, and yes these are important to me.'

Pabloo continued 'so what will be the measure of your success then?'

Rachel smiled and mentioned, 'I see where you are going. Now it is becoming clear.'

'Exactly! You need to establish your measure of success and work towards it. In that journey, you will link up to the key behaviors required for the role and eventually excel in an area of your interest. You can establish your goal statements and work towards it.'

Rachel sounded convinced and said 'I get it! But is it not that most of the time our behaviors get influenced by what is happening around us? And if that is the case how do we show consistency in the required behavior?'

'Fantastic question Rachel' said Pabloo almost instantaneously. 'To bring in consistency in your behavior you need to do critical reflection through a single loop, double loop and triple loop learning'.[27].

Before Pabloo could finish, Michael as always with his curiosity jumped into this with a grin 'critical? single, double, triple? I hope my daughter does not have to undergo any medical procedures.'

'Dad, I'm sure that you are aware a critical reflection process is a purposeful activity for making self-changes and improvements.'

'Well said Rachel, critical reflection makes us aware and eventually takes us to a stage of self-actualization, and before Michael asks what is

---

[27] Argyris, C. & Schon, D. (1978). Organizational Learning: A Theory of Action Perspective. Reading, Massachusetts: Addison-Wesley Publishing Co. & Mezirow, J. (1991). Transformative dimensions in adult learning. San Francisco: Jossey-Bass.

self-actualization – it is the realization or fulfillment of one's talents and potentialities, especially considered as a drive or zeal within oneself' explained Pabloo.

'Very interesting and what about the single, double and triple? asked Michael.

'Yes, even I have no clue about it' Rachel joined.

Pabloo added 'single, double and triple-loop learning are concepts in different methods of learning. While single-loop learning is just a change in behavior for the desired solution, double-loop and triple-loop learning are the abilities to question and examine the underlying principles of their belief system and enable them to shift in the context of their belief system.'

Rachel looked eager and asked, 'I would like to relate to it better. Can you give me an example of this in a workplace?'

'Well, let me try Rachel. Tell me one of the constant challenges for you at work?'

'Disagreements' Rachel answered almost immediately.

'All right, can you elaborate a little' asked Pabloo.

'Sure, you see, very often in the working environment that I'm in, we have this common trouble of agreeing to each other's point of view, though in the end we know we can make only one choice and usually it is not without much dissatisfaction or even resentfulness at times' Rachel elaborated.

'So how do you cope with that?' Pabloo asked quickly.

'It depends, when I do not have a choice, say for example, with a disagreement with my boss, then I usually simmer down to agree but at the same time given a choice and a situation where I do not feel the pressure of the hierarchy, I make my point put up strongly.'

Pabloo thought for a moment and said 'so, is it fair to say that you change your behavior based on the situation and the environment?'

'Yes' Rachel agreed.

Pabloo continued 'well Rachel, you just explained yourself the single loop learning.'

'Did I?' asked Rachel surprisingly.'

'Single loop learning is essentially an adjustment towards an outcome. In terms of behavior, it is a change in behavior for the desired outcome. In the context of the example you gave, you felt that you need to change the way that you react to the situation especially when you disagree with your boss. This happened because of your previous experience in such situations with your boss and you eventually learned a way to cope with it.'

'That is because I do not have a choice' Rachel explained.

'That is not because you do not have a choice, it is because you think you do not have a choice and that is where double-loop learning and triple-loop learning come in handy. It requires a shift in your thinking and learning to question the underlying reasons behind it and work towards it for an outcome'. 'Going back to the same example of disagreement with your boss, an approach towards double-loop learning would be to be able to genuinely see his perspective beyond your assumptions and belief system.'

Rachel looked concerned and mentioned 'I do that, but I simply cannot see his point.'

Pabloo said, 'as I mentioned earlier it requires a shift beyond your thinking of what you hold as true, and that is your belief.'

Michael intervened 'are you saying my daughter should give up her belief system to see someone else's perspective?'

'I am not saying she should give up Michael, I am just saying she should look beyond her own. As humans, we have evolved over thousands of years. What was considered to be true just about a couple of centuries before is being realized as not true now. If that can happen to humanity, then at an individual level, it would be best to keep learning than being struck with what you think alone is the truth.'

'Now that is philosophy!' said Michael smilingly.

Pabloo added 'let me put it this way, an individual belief system is built on experience and non-experience aspects of life. The experience aspect is based on certain situations and environments and may not necessarily be universal. The non-experience aspect is what was told to him/her all through life. Therefore you see both aspects can differ from person to person and therefore the belief system can also change from person to person. What may be right to an individual may not be right to another person.'

Rachel nodded, 'agree with your point but how does it solve my purpose to the example that I gave?'

Pabloo added, 'invite conversations which are outcome-based and importantly leave emotions out of it. Just because your boss has a counterargument does not mean he is incompetent or a bad person. He is just stating through his belief system, both experience and the non-experience aspects of it'. Rachel asked 'and what if the outcome is not adding up from his point of view?'

'Challenge it Rachel!' said Pabloo with higher energy. 'Please remember, some of the best ideas and HR interventions came because we challenged the obvious, questioned the average, and kept pushing for a greater outcome.'

Michael asked 'then what can possibly be triple-loop learning?'

'The basic of it would be learning how to learn. It is an approach through which you can develop innovative solutions to complex problems. It questions the fundamentals of the very basic foundation. To quote an example, it can be questioning why we would need double-loop learning and not some other alternatives. Why is anything considered right or wrong in the first place? It usually leads to a transformational change! As HR professionals, we have the responsibility of making these single, double and triple-loop learning not just as individual learning but as organizational-wide learning to bring consistency.'

Rachel said 'I really like this approach, but is there a systematic way I can use to re-look at my belief system?'

'The most appropriate way is through critical reflection. Another powerful way you can study this would be through the Transactional Analysis' mentioned Pabloo.

Rachel mentioned, 'I studied it also during my Master's.'

'There is a reason for them to add such important subjects to your course. Transactional analysis goes beyond the ego states and has a concept called life scripts. This states we wrote a script during our childhood and all that we are doing is to live the script through our life!' Pabloo explained.

Michael almost stood up and said 'what? Is that even possible...? what sort of mumbo jumbo is that?'

A People Conversation between a Baby Boomer, Gen X and Gen Y – Part 2

'It is no mumbo jumbo Michael, it is a vast subject within transactional analysis' said Pabloo smilingly.

'And I am ready to hear this one out, it sounds directly coming from a Harry Potter movie' mentioned Michael with a gleeful smile.

Rachel also smiled and said, 'I have read about transaction analysis, more as an understanding of ego states but I have not heard about life scripts.'

'Even I am familiar with the ego states concepts, is that not the parent, adult, and child egos?' asked Michael.

'Exactly Michael' said Pabloo and added 'Transactional analysis broadly is the social psychology developed by Eric Berne in the early 1960s. It is widely practiced in the field of therapy, counseling, education, organizational and personal development, etc[28]. Some of the key concepts of TA include, ego states, strokes, games people play, life scripts, I'm ok, you're ok, etc.'

Michael said with a grin 'and I'm not OK until you tell me about the life scripts.'

Pabloo smiled and said 'since both of you are familiar with ego states, I guess it will be easier to understand. You see, as children, we were told

---

[28] Berne,E., (1961), Transactional Analysis in Psychotherapy A Systematic Individual and Social Psychiatry, Souvenir Press.

by our parents and other people around us what this world is about. We, in turn, weaved our perceptions of ourselves around it and built our world into a narrative about what we can and will do.'

'So this is just a strong influence of someone around us in our childhood?' asked Rachel.

Pabloo replied 'it is much more than influence Rachel, in fact, we start to build our scripts as babies as a way of survival in this world. We write our own stories and we are probably not even aware that we wrote it. By the time you are 3 or 4, you have already completed the first draft and around 7 you have completed the entire story!'

Michael questioned, 'I just don't get it, how can we write a story without knowing it?'

'The story is written unconsciously and we invariably end up living the life of the story without even realizing it.'

Michael again asked, 'so what is that we write in this story of ours?'

Pabloo responded, 'Well, it depends on what you experienced during your childhood. The point is, unconsciously all the decisions you make are based on your script, be it the role you have taken in your life or your personal choices.'

Rachel thought for a second or two and asked, 'so if it is all written as the script by us, then what good is for us to do anyway now?'

Pabloo said, 'this awareness of life scripts can make you re-write them Rachel. It is this ability of you to do so that will change or transform your life forever! Now you cannot just do that sitting here right now, it is a process or a journey towards awareness and change. If this interests you, then you should definitely get into the field of transactional analysis or seek an expert's guidance.'

Michael asked, 'how should someone like me know this better?'

'Transactional analysis has a presence across the globe Michael. There are communities and chapters in almost all countries through the International Transactional Analysis Association. You just have to reach out to them.'

'I am going to do that, there are a few things that I would want to know about my script!' said Michael.

Rachel asked *'Pabloo, I wanted to ask you this. How do you handle organizational politics? To be honest with you, it is one of the reasons why I am thinking* of moving out of Human Resources and get into another field.'

Pabloo realized Rachel was starting to open up and her question posted is about the external environment. He mentioned, 'before I attempt to answer that question, I have a question for you. I wanted to know how organizational politics can be the reason for you to move out of HR. I am sure you agree it is prevalent in all the departments in an organization.'

'I agree' said Rachel, 'but the problem is, I have to lift an aggrieved employee who has been a victim of politics as part of my role in employee relations. It makes me unhappy that sometimes I cannot help such employees who reach out to me.'

'So it is your inability to help those employees at times that makes you sad, and not the profession, right?' asked Pabloo.

'You got that right! It is the inability. Personally, I love working with people.'

Pabloo looked straight into Rachel's eyes and asked 'If you love Human Resources, how can you leave those poor employees and think of walking away, I mean, where will they go? Let us try and fix it in some way so that they can continue to look up to the dependable and compassionate Rachel!' Rachel felt very responsible; it just touched her heart the way Pabloo put it across.

Organizational politics means, Mobilizing of Power within the organization. It happens when either individuals or groups claim the organization's resource-sharing system.[29]. Organizational politics are generated for various reasons: due to the history of past politics, external pressure from stakeholders, structural cleavages, and saliences of the issues, complexity, and uncertainty.'

Just then Rachel asked concernedly, 'can we stop organizational politics?'

'You cannot stop organizational politics. It is bound to happen in any organization because decisions about what strategy to determine are always political. The parties involved seek to legitimize the proposals, ideas, values and demands they espoused, whilst denying those which they seek to oppose.' Just then Pabloo's watch beeped, it was 9 PM already but the three of them were deeply involved in the conversation. Pabloo continued, 'there are many political games that will come to play in an organization. To quote a few - whistle-blowing, young turk games, rival camp games, empire building games, budgeting games, alliances games, etc.'

'Oh, I see. I did not know about so many details behind politics, I thought it usually crops because of an individual's greed or pride or even jealousy' Rachel quipped.

Pabloo answered, 'in a way if you look at it, what you said is right. Just that it can be more than one individual and many more reasons other than the three you have quoted.'

'You mean people as a group can gang up on an individual?'

'Yes Rachel, it is possible' said Pabloo 'although, I will not use the word ganging up. Let me try and explain this with an example. If you take the alliance games, it is usually played by more than one person. As the name suggests, this group is formed by people within an organization

---

[29] Pettigrew, A., (1973), The politics of Organizational decision-making, Tavistock.

who share a common interest and a goal. They usually play this game sometimes as a response to a threat or because the same resources are being shared. The most common alliance game would be the one played by peers at the same level seeking reciprocal support. The obvious reason is to protect the common interest and feel more secure in case of opposition. This risk of getting pointed out as an individual is reduced to a large extent as it is being played horizontally in the organization.'

Rachel nodded, 'okay. Also, Pabloo can you give me an example of an individual game played?'

Pabloo said, 'Budgeting game can be an example of that. It is played by an individual, usually a manager, to secure resources. Budgeting often has a clear rule and this game is about getting the most money a manager can typically get by asking for too much with the knowledge that you will get only a part of what you asked for. More than any other game, this is zero-sum, because when one manager gets the money, the other does not. This is a natural quality many managers exhibit and the most common reason is - the more money a manager has, the more he can spend or save. For eg: The higher the amount he can save, he is perceived to be an effective manager, and hence their position is much more secure. The size of the budget also matters as managers tend to link it to their ego about the value and beliefs of their role in the organization. This reinstates the power in their workplace.'

Rachel asked 'how do we handle it?'

'There are a few ways to handle it. For a budgeting game, the best approach would be to have a robust system that links the outcome with measurable components in place that reduces the opportunity to exhibit such qualities. And for an alliance game, an approach would be to identify the cause for the alliance being built. Similarly, for other games, there are specific approaches to tackle it. One thing for us to remember is such political games are not necessarily a bad thing as long as it is within limits.'

'So you are saying all these are good?' Rachel asked surprisingly.

'No' Pabloo replied firmly. *'I am just saying it is not a bad thing considering such games can sometimes be the harbinger of issues in the organization and as it is you cannot prevent them.'*

'Hmm' nodded Rachel, 'so what should be an overall approach to reduce it?' she asked further.

'Because Power and Politics are related to a large extent, as HR professionals it is our onus to bring in a culture where power is not being abused but used responsibly. We need to educate our workforce, and importantly our managers on this. A proven method for that would be through Pfeffer's 7 effective ways to use Power[30] explained Pabloo.

Michael mentioned, 'another seven? We are hitting the sevens very often.'

Pabloo continued 'Jeffrey Pfeffer, another brilliant mind in the field of organizational theory and human resource management pointed out the seven effective ways through which we can use Power effectively namely Goal, Individuals, Points of view, Other power bases, Your power bases, Strategies and Tactics and Actions. He states each of these can significantly help individuals and organizations to achieve great results in terms of higher performance. For eg, by establishing Goals, you can understand what we are trying to achieve in consultation with stakeholders. You can identify individuals, who are influential in achieving these goals. You can take the point of view of important people and understand both your and other members' power bases which can have an influence. You can also analyze whether the strategies and tactics are appropriate and take the ethical course of action.'

'And Rachel, as an HR, if you want to be a strategic player in reducing organizational politics, then you need to understand the internal political

---

[30]   Pfeffer, J., (2022), 7 Rules of Power – Surprising – But True – Advice on how to get things done and Advance your career, Swift Press.

structure of your organization with a correlation to how it can affect policies that you design. You also need to play a role of a conformist innovator which is to 'accept' the ends of the organization but to adjust the 'means' to achieve them. I personally feel such situations of politics should not sadden you; you should accept it as a way of the organization and importantly contribute by effective means to reduce its ill effects! Since your job involves more interaction with aggrieved employees, you need to exhibit a higher emotional intelligence.'

And just then Michael quipped, 'Emotional intelligence? You also mentioned it back in the college as a response to one of the questions by a student. So I wanted to ask you what it is all about? I know it is about emotions but what about the intelligence part?'

'Emotional intelligence is the ability to perceive accurately, appraise and express emotions.[31]. *It is an important aspect of both your social and self-awareness & management. It is a way through which you recognize, understand, and manage your own emotions and also recognize, understand, and influence the emotions of others. As an HR professional, this works clearly to your advantage in a working environment as you make much more meaningful conversations with others in* the form of effective conversations, empathize and establish healthier relationships. At a self-level, once you are aware of your emotions, you will be able to drive and propel for greater fulfillment in your life and not be saddened or become a victim of your emotional state of mind' explained Pabloo.

'Now I know how Judy gets the better of me every time' said Michael jokingly.

Rachel asked 'how do we develop greater emotional intelligence? I know I can increase it by critical reflection within me, but how do I develop it for others?' Pabloo acknowledged Rachel's true HR quality of going beyond her interest in herself for others.

---

[31] Mayer, J., Brackett, M., & Salovey, P., (2004), Emotional Intelligence, Dude Pub.

'There are many ways to do it. One proven successful way is through Coaching. You can coach other people on the aspects of emotional intelligence.'

Michael said, 'Coach? Can't we just simply tell them?'

'Coaching differs from telling people. Coaching is a process in which one individual, the coach, creates a co-creating relationship with others that makes it easier for them to learn.[32] *In a way, if you look at it, as a coach, you partner with someone in a thought-provoking and creative process that inspires them to maximize their personal and professional potential, which is particularly important in today›s uncertain and complex environment.*'

'Well, I should say these things now have changed. Those days when I was young, at work, we were just told what to do and we just followed it' added Michael.

Pabloo smiled and mentioned 'as we discussed earlier, you would fall under the Baby Boomers era, Michael. The key drivers for work engagement and the techniques that were used at that time were entirely different'.'

'Can you please tell me a little more about the coaching part? How do I coach another person on EI or for that matter in anything?' asked Rachel.

'There are many coaching techniques that you can employ. A popular and simplest technique would be the GROW model.[33] Through this coaching model when you engage as a coach with another person in different stages of your coaching conversation, you can encourage the other person to establish a Goal statement (G), make them look at

---

[32] Drake, D., Spence, G., & Bachkirova, T., (2016), The SAGE Handbook of Coaching, SAGE Publications.

[33] Whitmore, J., (1993), Coaching for Performance – A Practical guide for Growing your Own Business, John Wiley & Sons.

where they are currently with the respect to the Goal, in other words, Reality (R). Then, enable them to look at various ways to choose the right path toward the goal, in other words, Options (O) and finally towards the implementation plan or the Way forward (W).'

Michael asked curiously, 'but how do we do all of these without telling? I can understand the goal part but for the other stages, you still have to tell, Right?'

'The essence of coaching is not telling! As I said earlier, it should be a thought-provoking process. There are ways through which you can learn this art of coaching. The international coaching federation with a presence in close to 140 countries accredits coaching programs for those who are interested' answered Pabloo.

'Wow, the world has changed! We live in exciting times. I wish I can get benefitted from all of these. In all honesty, what I got was an opportunity to be only a Mentor' said Michael.

Pabloo mentioned, 'Michael, you can get hugely benefitted from Mentoring.'

'I am aware, it is a fulfilling experience to guide the youngsters but what I was speaking about is, if I can get an opportunity to get benefitted from the current realities.'

Pabloo thought for a while and mentioned, 'Have you considered reverse mentoring?' Michael looked clueless. Pabloo continued 'Reverse mentoring[34] is a method of pairing older members with the younger ones to mentor them on topics such as technology, social media, etc.'

'Is that even in practice?'

'Yes, Michael' said Pabloo. 'Organizations have started to realize the benefits of reverse mentoring. Gen Y or Millennials are currently close

---

[34] Murphy, W.M., (2012), Reverse mentoring at work: Fostering cross-generational learning and developing millennial leaders, Wiley online library, Citations: 144.

to 40 to 45% of the global workforce, and their ideas and knowledge are proving to be very useful for older employees, especially on the current trends. Some of the key overall benefits include new perspectives and improved innovation, more effective strategic plans, improved knowledge transfer (in both directions), reduced 'generation gap', and recognition of better leadership skills in younger employees.'

'I agree' said Michael, 'the youngsters in this generation are extremely smart and I like this idea of reverse mentoring, I do not mind implementing this in my college. The professors can get benefitted.'

Rachel asked 'Pabloo, one of the constant concerns that we have from the employees in our organization is that the management is a little rigid. My organization has a mixture of all three generations. Understandably, the leadership positions are filled by Gen X or Baby Boomers, middle management is slowly making way for Gen Y but we have a considerable amount of workforce at the junior management and at the agent level which is again Gen Y and Gen Z. As an employee's relations person, I constantly get concerns from the employees about the rules of the organization. Though I have brought this up to the notice of the management, there has been no greater progress in that aspect. Sometimes I wonder if they are deliberately avoiding it. Tell me about your viewpoints on this and is it common in your country too?'

Pabloo replied, 'before I comment on that, I would like to know what exactly the complaints from these employees are?'

'Grievances like how they find it difficult working under the supervision and complying with rules. While it is not exactly a bureaucratic organization but I guess they want a little more freedom. My point is, it is understandable that they prefer it and I stand as an example for the preference, Why is the management not doing much about it?' Rachel answered.

'It seems to be the preference of certain management in organizations. Even back in my country, we have many such organizations which still have classic structures and processes. There can be many reasons for it, but one of the strongest reasons is the control system.'

Michael asked 'Control? Is that even the right thing for them to do? Why would they control?'

Pabloo added further, 'Central to their purpose is managerial control within the organizations linked with an ideology of progress. Control is used to circumscribe idiosyncratic behavior to conform to the rational plan of the organization.[35] Such a classical approach gives them a form of control through agency theory – Fulfilling the contractual obligation, performance and evaluation – What is agreed to what is achieved, Clan control – Working with close supervision and complying with rules. This way, a clearly defined boundary is established, unlike the modern way of the boundary-less concept of the new forms of organizations. There can also be other reasons for it such as the orientation and ownership of the organization. Orientation relates to the basic goals of the organization and ownership is who legally owns them and their values. The owners may not necessarily be in favor of a flexible model, adding to this, the kind of industry, size, and type. Inertia sets in the way of their preference and if it works, organizations remain classically structured. But Rachel, as an HR person, you need to continue your efforts to bring it to the notice of your management. I think it is important for a reason, Gen Y and Gen Z will be more than 50% of the global workforce by 2025 and they prefer a certain degree of flexibility. An organization that does not realize this might lose its edge given the realities. They have to wake up to the new forms of organization.'

'What should I propose as an alternate?' asked Rachel.

'You have many other new forms of organization to choose from, but it has to be done after careful consideration. You would agree you cannot change management style overnight!' answered Pabloo.

---

[35] Tannenbaum, A. S., & Georgopoulos, B. S. (1957). The distribution of control in formal organizations. Social Forces, 36, 44–50.

Michael asked 'What is this new form of organization? Are we doing away with employment on the whole? What exactly is it?'

All three of them were engrossed in the conversation and suddenly heard a voice from behind, 'Do you realize that Pabloo has to go back to the hotel?'

The three of them turned around to see Judy. Michael quickly responded, 'oh! my bad, I did not realize that.'

'You still realize we should take care of our guest, right?' said Judy smilingly.

Pabloo smiled and responded, 'thanks Judy, the three of us were enjoying a nice conversation, I think we should be done in a bit.'

'As long as you are fine Pabloo' Judy said smilingly and walked back inside.

'There you go, what I told you about her emotional intelligence?' quipped Michael.

Rachel smiled and said, 'now coming back to our conversation, what are the new forms of organization Pabloo?'

A People Conversation between a Baby Boomer, Gen X and Gen Y – Part 3

P abloo said, 'New forms of organizations started to arise as a reaction to bureaucracy initially, and later there was a shift to search for managing organizational change and dealing with the speed of change in contemporary societies. One important driver for that was the claim that stability in an organization and society is no longer the norm and that change is endemic in the contemporary world. Some examples of new forms of organization are Technocracy, Adhocracy, Virtual Organization, etc. These organizations differ in the way of hierarchies being flat, authority being more distributive, and division of labor through less specialization and expanded job roles, and rules being more discretionary and relationship based. These new forms of organizations are well supported by technology, thanks to the ability of ICTs to integrate into computers, teleworking, communication, etc. In addition, the Human Resources of these organizations operate with a certain degree of flexibility, which also seems to be working well, especially with Gen Y or Millennial workforce.'

Michael asked, 'You keep talking about flexibility, what exactly is that?'

'Flexibility is identified in order to cope with change. It covers both short-term responsiveness and long-term agility.[36] Broadly four main types of flexibility were identified: task or functional flexibility:

---

[36] Boxall, P.F., and Purcell, J. (2003), Strategy and Human Resource Management, Palgrave Macmillan.

where employees may be multi-skilled. numerical flexibility: using different types of employment contracts and subcontracting. temporal flexibility: where the number and pattern of hours worked varies, for example, zero hours, and annual hours. wage flexibility: where wages are individualized and may be performance-related[37] explained Pabloo.

'How does this flexibility gets translated into HR policies? Basically, how does HR get the buying from the management?' asked Rachel.

Pabloo replied, 'flexible policies include a range of benefits to be truly irresistible. Obviously, the pay component would play an important role. Other benefits may include personal development in all its forms. A pleasant working environment is another feature, as is outstanding facility and equipment. An important factor would be a culture that is democratic that provides employees with plenty of autonomy. Now the buying part from the management is not going to be easy. it is understandable if the management becomes apprehensive given the size of the responsibility but that's exactly where you need to present the reality to your management as an HR professional. One way of doing it can be through business cases with data. Your current employee satisfaction and engagement levels, attrition levels, performance output, etc. are all the key indicators of the current health of your workforce. You need to showcase the benefits of this flexibility linking up to these indicators or levers for a progressive positive outcome and that is how you build a smart and agile workforce.'

Rachel nodded and asked 'Pabloo, I would also like to know from you that out of all the qualities that we spoke about for being a successful HR professional, what according to you would be the most important quality?'

'For me it is motivation! HR is all about development and not maintenance. In today's world of globalization, there persist volatility, uncertainty, complexity and ambiguity (VUCA) and as HR professionals

---

[37] Morris, J., Blyton, P., (1991), A Flexible Future? - Prospects for Employment and Organization, de Gruyter.

it is our responsibility to motivate our workforce to deal with these components and achieve greater heights effectively.'

'Thanks, Pabloo!' Rachel added, 'it is so much of a HR saying that money is not a motivator! Therefore my question is what are the effective motivational methods and channels? I know we spoke some bit of it in AI but what more in specific?'

Pabloo looked at Rachel and said, 'firstly, I do not agree with the saying 'Money is not a motivator', It clearly is! There are no questions about it. It is just that it is not the only motivator. There are many other motivators that broadly fall under intrinsic and extrinsic motivation. But before we get into it, as HR we need to make a clear distinction between content and process theories of motivation.'

Rachel looked clueless and asked Pabloo instantaneously, 'Oh, what are those?'

'A content theory[38] focuses on what (outcome or reward) motivates people. In contrast, process theories[39] concentrate on how people are motivated, or the cognitive process used to connect effort with outcomes or rewards' explained Pabloo.

'Wow, I like the distinction. Tell me a little more about it, Pabloo' said Rachel.

Pabloo continued, 'Well content theory is pretty straightforward, as mentioned earlier, it is concerned with individual needs and goals, outcomes or rewards. Some of the well-known content motivation theories include the two-factor theory by Herzberg and the hierarchy of needs theory by Maslow.'[40].

---

[38] Maslow, H.A., (1981), Motivation And Personality, Harper & Row.

[39] Adams, J. S. (1963). Towards an understanding of inequity. The Journal of Abnormal and Social Psychology, 67(5), 422–436.

[40] Herzberg, F., (1968), One more time - How do you motivate Employees, Harvard Business Review & Maslow, A. H. (1943). A theory of human motivation. Psychological Review, 50, 370–396.

Michael said, 'Yes, even I'm familiar with Maslow's theory of hierarchy.'

Pabloo explained further, 'For the process theory of motivation, the best example that I can think of is expectancy theory, which states the force of the motivation is a combination of expectancy, instrumentality, and valence.'

Michael smiled and said 'ahem, in English please!'

Pabloo quickly continued 'expectancy is a belief that extra effort will result in better performance. Instrumentality is a belief that better performance will lead to rewards. Valence is perceived as the value of the reward[41]. Now as HR professionals, we should realize both content and process motivations are not opposite but complimentary. Therefore our job does not only involve a good reward and recognition system but also creating the right atmosphere and the required mindset.'

'Oh okay! Got it' said Rachel.

Michael asked, 'so what is intrinsic and extrinsic motivation then?

'Intrinsic motivation is the spontaneous satisfaction individuals derive from the activity itself. Extrinsic motivation, in contrast, requires tangible or verbal rewards.'

'Thanks, Pabloo, so which is better intrinsic or extrinsic?'

Pabloo responded, 'both have their merits and de-merits, though it is a well-known fact that intrinsic rewards have more long-term results including more engaged and committed employees. Perhaps as an approach, we can consider the stages of employees' career development.'

Michael asked inquisitively 'stages?'

---

[41] Palmer, T. M., & Barnett, A.G., (1998), Mutual Influence in Interpersonal Communication Theory and Research in Cognition, Affect, and Behavior, Ablex Publishing Corporation.

'Yes, stages' mentioned Pabloo and continued, 'There are five stages that are identified broadly as career development stages[42] and it is linked with the life-span approach to career choice and adaptation. The five stages are Growth, Exploration, Establishment, Maintenance and Decline. It is important to note that within each of these five individual stages, there will be phases such as adolescence, early adulthood, and middle and late adulthood. Also, in each of these phases within a stage the preferences of an individual change with time and experience based on their life situations. Since you mentioned your organization is having three generations of the workforce, it might be a useful concept for you to explore.'

Michael further asked 'all these stages, phases, intrinsic, extrinsic, and content and process theories are too much for me to grasp. Can you tell me a simple but effective way to motivate people?'

'Sure! You can use strokes to motivate others and even yourself.'

Michael said smilingly 'another concept?'

'It is a simple but an effective way to recognize both other people and self; in other words, a stroke is a unit of attention that provides stimulation to an individual.'[43]

'And how do we exactly stroke?' asked Michael curiously.

'Strokes can be both verbal and non-verbal. It can be anything from a simple hello to a full-length conversation. It can also be a handshake or a smile, a compliment, or for that matter even a frown, all are ways of stroking' explained Pabloo.

'A frown?'

'Yes Rachel, even a frown, you see, any stroke is better than no stroke at all. If you apply this concept as an HR person, you will realize it

---

[42] Greenhaus, J., & Callanan, G. (1994), Career management, Fort Worth: Dryden.

[43] Woollams, S., & Brown, M., (1978), Transactional Analysis. MIcooper: Stan Woollams.

is nothing but how you engage with your employees in relationship building. Researchers are continuously pointing out how employees crave recognition however small, be it. You can use these strokes for the process of motivation, as strokes reinforce behavior.'

Rachel asked again, 'how does it reinforce behavior?'

Pabloo continued, 'there is a science behind it and it is supported through research conducted on two sets of babies. The first set of babies are those reared in a children's home and the second set are those raised in families. The first set, though fed well, was kept clean and warm but experienced physical and emotional difficulties compared to other babies reared by their mothers. This is because the babies in the children's' home lacked stimulation. They had little to look at all day except the white walls of their rooms. Above all, they had less physical contact with those caretakers. They lacked touching, cuddling, and stroking. As grown-ups, we still crave physical contact. But we also substitute other forms of recognition in place of physical touching. These substitutes are verbal and non-verbal strokes. It is popularly known as recognition-hunger, which describes our need for this kind of acknowledgment by others.'

'It's simply amazing!' said Michael with wide eyes. 'I did not know there was so much to even to a simple nod and how it can make an impact.'

'Absolutely Michael and with simple cues and gestures you can make a whole lot of difference.'

Rachel asked, 'but Pabloo I am still not clear how it reinforces behavior in an office environment.'

'Yeah sorry, I missed that part' continued Pabloo *'you can reinforce the much-needed positive behavior through positive strokes. It is the one through which the receiver experiences pleasantness. As we know, it has a cascading effect. Pleasant experiences bring happiness within themselves/ individuals and this in turn reinforces positive behavior.'*

'So are you saying that we should keep giving positive strokes as much as possible? Rachel asked further.

'Yes Rachel!' said Pabloo almost instantaneously 'although we should be truthful and sincere while we give that, and just do not say something for the sake of it, a plastic stroke. For it to be genuine, you need to know about the individuals and their unique qualities which are directly linked to building a relationship with employees.›

'I agree!' said Rachel, 'but I have another question for you, through positive strokes you may acknowledge an individual's unique quality as a way of motivation, but how do we know if the person is ready for the next level for the quality complimented or skill or anything for that case? I know we spoke about coaching, but how do we know if there is a risk of the individual not even willing or being able to scale up and how should we approach it from an HR professional standpoint?'

Pabloo nodded and said, 'so Rachel, on the will part, as HR professionals, our approach should be to treat all individuals equally but at the same time acknowledge that each of them can have unique strengths. If some individuals are not willing to have the right mindset required, we cannot force them, we can only inspire them. End of the day, individuals have free will and choices. Regarding the skill part, you would agree coaching can go a long way and as HR professionals we can determine the right training interventions that are needed both for individuals and teams or groups. On those same lines, a management tool was developed called a Skill/Will matrix.[44] A four-quadrant approach was presented in terms of Ability (skill) and Desire (will). In that model- Directing was given as an approach towards staff members with low skills and low will, Supporting for low skill and high will, Coaching for high skill and low will, and finally Delegating as an approach for staff members who have high skills and high will.'

---

[44] Landsberg, M., (1997) The Tao of Coaching - Boost Your Effectiveness at Work by Inspiring and Developing Those Around You. (Santa Monica, CA: Knowledge Exchange, 1997).

'So there is a prescriptive way to approach these then. It is good to note that there are so many options to choose from. Back in my days, I remember there was a concept called ZPD which was used in the educational space' said Michael.

Pabloo responded, 'Well it is still being employed, although there has been the development of ZPD into scaffolding.' Michael looked surprised that Pabloo was aware of ZPD.

Rachel on the other hand mentioned jokingly 'and I have no clue about what you both are speaking about.'

Pabloo mentioned, 'ZPD means Zonal Proximal Development[45] which refers to the difference between what a learner can do without help and what he or she can do with the assistance of a skilled partner, let's say a adult guidance or peer guidance as an example. I think this model is more prominent in the educational space as a framework for development.'

Rachel asked intently 'can you give an example for me to place this better in a corporate setting?'

Pabloo said, 'Sure! Peer coaching[46] can be an example of this. It recognizes the importance of partners and other managers at the same level of work. Peer coaching is unique because of the mutuality and reciprocity of the relationship between one person and at least one other. This relationship is based on partnership and equality that removes the objective difference which is power, salary, and status.'

'There is so much HR does and can do. I am thinking of changing my career to HR' said Michael smilingly.

---

[45] Vygotsky, L. S. (1978). Mind in society: The development of higher psychological processes Cambridge, Mass.: Harvard University Press.

[46] Parker, P., Hall, D. T., & Kram, K. E. (2008). Peer coaching: A relational process for accelerating career learning. Academy of Management Learning & Education, 7, 487-503.

Rachel on the other hand mentioned, 'I still cannot figure out why HR is so underrated despite all the good things that we get into the organization. I think it is just unfair!'

Michael looked at Pabloo and asked 'do you agree to this, Pabloo?'

Pabloo said, 'Well to some extent Michael, yes! But at the same time, I should say that organizations are waking up to the power of Human Resources. One of the reasons that HR was traditionally underrated is because business is driven by profit motives while HR takes the role of being the agent of morality driven by ethical practices. This does cause conflict between Business and HR.'

Michael interrupted and asked, *'what is this ethical aspect of HR?'*

'HR take a standpoint, being profitable is a virtue of business organizations but it is not their only virtue. Though part of HR people's practices stems from legal requirements – such as employment, law, health, safety, and consumer protection, part of this responsibility is being moral and ethical.[47]. Simply put - ethics is a set of principles that is defined as a code and acts as a guide to conduct. Moral, in contrast, is concerned with the actions of the individual to live to the demands of what is perceived as right.[48]. Now, I am not saying business wants unethical practices, I am just saying business priorities sometimes take over HR people practices. Having said that, lately businesses have started to realize the potential of HR through its service delivery mechanism such as Business partners, Centre of Excellence, Shared Services, etc.[49] In fact, for me, HR's contribution goes beyond the

---

[47] Kaptein, M. & Wempe, J., (1998), The Ethics Report: A means of sharing responsibility, Business Ethics A European Review 7(3):131-139.

[48] Lawton, A. (1999), Ethics and Management. In A. Rose & A.Lawton (Eds.), Public service management (pp.299-300), Harlow, UK:Prentice Hall.

[49] Ulrich, D., (1997), Human Resource Champions: The next agenda for adding value and delivering results. Harvard Business Press, Cambridge, MA, ISBN: 9780875847191, Pages: 281.

organization and reaches the overall country's economic development including its Socio-cultural, Environmental and Ethical aspects.'

'And how do you justify the statement you just made?' asked Michael curiously.

'I am very confident of it' said Pabloo, 'at least from my country's perspective. Here is why I say this broadly under four points.

First, the Indian government recognizes the role of the private sector in its Tiger economic policies. The Private sector's contribution is as high as three-fourths of the overall GDP. HR plays a pivotal role in building the private sector workforce broadly from an ability, motivation and opportunity standpoint, be it through best practices or best-fit models. So, HR's efforts in hiring the right talents, developing them, and creating a high-performance culture are directly linked to the development of the country's economic development at some level. The higher the efforts put in, the greater the overall economic output will be in the form of goods and services.

Second, between the two contrarian views of people who are selfish, acquisitive, and aggressive by nature v/s people who are moral, reasonable, and capable of self-governance, effective HR believes in the latter. They set precedence through people practices, instilling values and inspiring individuals to be socially and morally responsible. Responsible behavior translates to responsible individuals. Such individuals translate greater positive energy into their approach and actions. This in turn, reduces social inequality and thinner disparity, in other words, a happier society! It is this joy quotient that translates to contentment and positivity and has its effect on the overall consumerism and secularism of the country.

Third, one of the key concerns that the world is facing now - is pollution and other harmful effects of industrial and technological development. HR through its multiple initiatives such as CSR, etc tries to mitigate these negative effects by collaborating with the business and the principal shareholders - be it to reduce the carbon footprint or to take up GO green initiatives. According to one report, in India, the total contribution through CSR (Corporate Social Responsibility) in 2014-15 is a whopping 4,368 crore rupees by over 460 companies.[50] HR in collaboration with the management makes a difference to the society by recommending the right causes to fund - be it rural development, promoting education, or any other philanthropic initiative. The real bottom line is that it touches the lives of millions of people for a greater and brighter tomorrow! The other way of looking at this is that HR contributes to innovation, brand building and long-term thinking through CSR initiatives.

Fourth and final, HR plays a key role in transforming the knowledge and skills landscape of the country to make India a superpower. The workforce demographics have a steady increase in the young labor force in the country. This is of huge significance to India, considering many developed countries are facing an aging population. India on the other hand, will have one of the highest young human capital pools for building a greater economy. While this works in our favor, the leaders need to prepare Gen Y and Gen Z to take greater responsibilities. HR plays a transformational role in creating the leaders of tomorrow, be it the transfer of knowledge and skills from Baby Boomers and Gen X to Gen Y and Z or promoting younger leadership at the board level through mentoring programs or engaging the younger workforce through flexible HR policies or promoting diversity and inclusion or by promoting women in leadership to counter the glass ceiling, and I can keep going on!

Rachel was happy and suddenly was proud of herself for performing the role of HR. She never in the past thought how much Human Resource contributes to the economy and society. She started to respect the profession even more and was eager to get similar data related to her

---

[50] Bhaduri,N.S. & Selarka, E. (2016), Corporate Governance and Corporate Social Responsibility of Indian Companies, Springer Singapore (ebook).

very own country. She quipped with utmost joy *'Thanks Pabloo! There is no doubt in my mind now and I am clear that I wanted to excel in the field of Human Resources. I will take any challenge as an opportunity to learn and keep moving upward in my journey as an HR Leader'.*

'Excellent' said Pabloo, 'as long as you do not keep your focus on performance goal orientation but a learning goal orientation, your journey will be successful.'

Rachel blinked for a moment, Pabloo quickly added 'the former is the seeking by individuals to show and prove that their competencies are adequate by avoiding negative judgments in favor of positive ones. Learning goal orientation, on the other hand, is the willingness of individuals to develop new skills and master new situations. Enjoy this learning journey!'

Looking at Rachel's smile and excitement about the profession that she loved, Michael looked happy and like any father, he was gleaming with pride.

Pabloo looked at his watch and said, 'Well guys it is quite late, let me head back to the hotel. I have an exciting day in front of me tomorrow as we are visiting another country Bratislava.'

Rachel smiled and said, 'it is Slovakia; the capital of the country is Bratislava.'

'Oh my bad, got it' said Pabloo with a smile.

'It is a nice drive from here just over a couple of hours. Enjoy the trip' added Rachel.

'So, are we catching up tomorrow?' Michael asked.

'Well I am doubtful as once we are back we have planned to take a cruise in the Danube river' said Pabloo.

'Nice! In that case, can we catch up the day after?'

'Sure, Michael! Maybe we should meet at the same place where we met on the first day; incidentally, it is the last day of my trip here in Europe. We will catch up around 9 PM?'

'Fine with me' smiled Michael and asked further, 'well, now is there anything I can help you with?'

'Yes, you can drop me back to the hotel' said Pabloo with a smile.

The Fourth Day - A Discussion with the Ceo

Pabloo's alarm buzzed in his ears sharply by 6 AM in the hotel room. With just only a few hours of sleep, he was tempted to sleep a little more. But his enthusiasm got the better of him and he got off the bed. In about an hour or so, he met all his colleagues at the breakfast table.

'So guys, it is a nice day in front of us' said Singh. 'We are going to take a coach ride to Slovakia and once we are back in the evening we have planned a cruise ride on the river Danube.'

They all boarded the bus in about 45 minutes. Pabloo took the last row as he was still feeling a little tired. The bus started and in about 30 minutes Pabloo observed the lovely landscape of Europe. It was a beautiful view with lush greenery all around. He also noticed the speckled roads and the good lane discipline observed by all the drivers. He was admiring the lovely view from the window when he heard someone asking, so how do you like Europe?' Pabloo turned around and was not able to believe his eyes, it was Marshal Gold Smith, the world's top executive coach.

'Do you know who am I?' asked Marshal.

Pabloo who was still shocked said in a shaky voice, 'who would not know the world's highest-paid coach? What are you doing here? asked Pabloo.

'I am on a world tour and on my way to Bratislava. I heard you are in Europe so dropped by to say hi to you'.

Pabloo said in disbelief 'me? But how did you know me?'

'There was a write-up about you in the local journal and the word spreads out when a global HR leader visits Europe!'

Pabloo murmured 'err, well you know.'

Marshal asked, 'did you meet Dave Ulrich lately? I heard he is in Europe too'.

Now Pabloo's interest was more than ever. Dave Ulrich is one of the most influential HR Leaders. 'No' said Pabloo.

'Would you want me to arrange a meeting?' asked Marshal

'Yes' said Pabloo with excitement, 'I will give up anything to meet him.'

'........Pabloo, wake up man, you have been snoring for more than an hour now' said a familiar voice. 'Remember, we have a conversation to catch up with'.

Pabloo woke up in rush and saw Singh standing next to him. 'Get up please and come sit by my side' said Singh as he walked back to his seat. Pabloo in a half-sleep state nodded. It took him a few seconds to realize the dream he had. How much he wants to meet all the great leaders and murmured 'one day I will meet them and it is not too far' he told himself and stood up to join Singh.

'So tell me Pabloo, What is this about HR department should be in the roles of an independent body, I'm quite curious' asked Singh.

'HR can sometimes be caught up between management and people practice. Most often, HR has to succumb to the pressure of the management. Now if this has to change, then HR should be an independent entity with no pressures whatsoever. If that has to happen, then it will not be a bad idea for HR to operate as an independent body even for the private sectors' explained Pabloo.

'But it does to a large extend isn't it, I mean through your statutory compliances there is a strict monitor system from the labor department to adherence.'

'Yes, Singh but these compliances do not affect decisions taken through the course of business. What I mean is, it cannot have an impact on the need for ethical HR practices. Even HR as a department or the Head HR as an individual will have to think of their job security and they do not want to lock horns with the management, at least beyond a certain point.'

Singh said, 'agree to some extent, so what is your proposal then?'

Pabloo added 'the Head of HR should not be in the roles of the company. He/she should be a representative of a Global HR body that governs the ethical people practice of the organization, if not global at least national. A qualified Head of HR should be nominated by the National HR body to head an organization. He/She should get a tenure of 4 years in an organization and will have to drive its workforce for higher performance. He/she should be represented in the board meetings not just as the head of HR of a company but as a responsible leader keeping in mind the overall development of the country. They should be given authority to take decisions considering the interest of all the stakeholders and can report any sort of resistance from the management to the governing body. Among other responsibilities, one of the key tasks would be to report the best practices of the organization, along with other HR heads, to the National body and importantly what is lacking in the organization. The national HR body can bring in many regulations from this learning, especially from the private sector aspect.

Singh interrupted and chuckled, 'sounds like the HR regime to me.'

Pabloo continued unperturbed, 'this National HR body can work very closely with the government on key issues related to employability and national training policies.'

'How does it connect?' asked Singh.

'One of the biggest problems our country facing today is, in fact, many others as well, is that in the national skill base, there is a link between a failing education system and economic prosperity. Organizations are facing a shortage of skills and employability factors. With private organizations contributing to three-fourths of the overall GDP, it is clear that without further investment in education and skills, our economy will stand to lose the race of becoming a wealthy one. This much-needed input can be provided by the National HR body, thanks to the HR heads' explained Pabloo.

Singh said, 'it is still happening currently through the Ministry of Human Resource Development'.

'But the representation of private sectors HR is limited in that and my proposal has an overall linkage to the country's economy through Human Capital Investment.'

'Hmm' said Singh, 'also, what is with the four-year tenure?'

'HR heads should be challenged to bring up the organizations in these CXO four years' time. Their performance and success should be measured year on year and should be documented with the national HR body. This way, you promote HR leaders to constantly innovate and find ways to work closely with well-complimented people practices. Eventually, you can bring in uniformity and set standards. All of these will have a direct positive impact on the country's economy.' After the explanation, Pabloo paused for a moment and asked 'so, what do you think Singh?'

'Sure, it sounds revolutionary but how far it is practical and realistic is a question to be answered. That being said, it is a start and I think it is important.'

Pabloo nodded, 'Thank you, Singh, yes, we need to start somewhere, and now is the time. Obviously, we need to work on many details to present such an idea to a larger group and clearly, it might not go well with the CXOs.'

Singh nodded, 'Yes, I agree. The CXOs might be constrained by the regulation of the governing body. You see Pabloo, the job of the CXOs is highly pressurizing given the market competition and the growing rate of change in the business environment. They need to have complete freedom in the way they wanted to operate.'

'I agree but the reality is not helping organizations and the national economy.'

Singh looked confused and asked, 'I beg your pardon, Pabloo? Are you saying CXOs are not adding value?'

Pabloo elucidated, 'oh no no, all I am saying is there is a lot of scope for improvement for CXOs to add more value. To quote an example, despite the economic downturn, the value of top-level packages continues to climb and the gap between the pay of the average worker and that of a CXO seems to be ever-widening. The CIPD and High Pay Centre point out that if FTSE 100 CEO pay continues to increase at the same rate for the next 20 years as it has for the last two decades, the average ratio between CXO and average pay would increase from about 129:1 to more than 400:1.[51] In our country specifically, a huge pay gap between CXOs and other employees has come to the fore, with the biggest listed blue-chip firms doling out to their top executives' salary packages up to 1,200 times their median employee remunerations.'

Singh asked sharply, 'what is your point?'

Pabloo responded, 'the point is, all this has an impact on the country's economy at some level in the form of production of goods and services and there is very little an HR head can do in the current scheme of things given that there is an increased pressure upon him to pay out more incentives to the top management and the justification for the same is put as the need to retain the latter. In reality, such gaps can cause a huge demotivation among the workforce. In other words, we are engaging the HR head to do something against the very basic HR

---

[51] Gabaix, X. & Landier, A. (2008), Why has CEO pay increased so much? Quarterly Journal of Economics 123 (1): 49-100.

good practice. Such things can be averted through the model that I have proposed. Since the HR head has to report to the National HR body, a lot of regulations can come into play such as the CXOs salary cannot exceed 7 times the median salaries of the workforce. And this is just one among the many other such initiatives he can bring In.'

Singh had a smile on his face and mentioned, 'you are surely going to become unpopular among the top management with such ideas Pabloo.'

'Well, it is just an idea chief. I keep telling myself as HR we should keep flowing with ideas. If to implement it or not is a different story altogether.'

'We are here!' and just then said the tour guide. 'We have reached Bratislava!'

Hello Slovakia

Bratislava - the capital of Slovakia is another beautiful place in Europe. It was between Austria and Hungary surrounded by beautiful vineyards, small hills, and mountains. Castles, cathedrals, and churches are worth seeing in this fantastic city. After a guided tour of close to 3 hours, the entire team dropped by a local restaurant for lunch exclusively blocked for this team.

As everyone settled for lunch, Singh caught the attention of the team, 'well folks, this is an extended lunch session for a couple of hours. I was hoping to have a free-wheeling session with all of you about some important changes and focus that we can bring into our organization. As we look forward to a great year ahead of us, this session can be a start. As I said, it is a free-wheeling session, let's discuss anything that we think should be brought in. There will be no judgments here and there is no need to impress me or anyone, as this session will not be taken into consideration for your performance review' he said with a smile.

A mild laughter followed. Pabloo thought whether this session has anything to do with the conversation he had with the CEO on the bus. 'If it is, then well done' he told himself, 'I have managed to influence or kindle the creative dimension of a fellow leader, a key quality of any professional HR.'

After silence for about close to a minute, Khan, the Technology head stood up and asked, 'though we are a product-based company, I think we have not fully embraced technology as part of our organization. The world is moving to the next level of technology, be it Nano-technology,

Robotics, Transport, or just about anything. Who would have thought flying by the wire or Dial in Bus is even possible about a couple of decades ago. Therefore, if technology is a fast game changer, then we need to be a far more tech-driven company in all our strengths.'

The sales head, Shiva in agreement said, 'I completely agree with Khan. We should focus a lot more on Automation. It will help us in reducing human errors and increase greater productivity. In fact in my opinion we should automate everything and eliminate human intervention.'

The quality head, Aarthi, brought in a perspective, 'while there is no question about becoming fully automated, it makes me wonder to realize a world without human intervention. For me, human intervention is always needed, if not how do we challenge individuals to reach greater heights or promote innovation? And yes this is coming from the quality head herself. If everything is automated, then how do we differentiate both internally and externally?'

Shiva interrupted and said, 'Aarthi, are you saying the Google and Amazons of the world have not differentiated themselves?' The group got more involved in the conversation, there was a range of opinions and suggestions from everyone as to how the organizations should change focus and direction. For the next hour, it moved from one topic to another covering market, people, cost, brand, competition, and even the next elections! Throughout the discussion Pabloo was quiet, taking some notes. He was aware that this is a rich conversation and as an HR leader if he needs to bring change in the organization then the efforts should be complimentary to many of the points being mentioned here. At the same time, he was also wondering how would it be possible to have all these leaders focus on a single direction given the diverse set of ideas that they have.'

As he was wondering, Singh called out 'Pabloo, what do you think?'

Pabloo looked at his notes and then looked up and mentioned, 'firstly, I wanted to acknowledge some rich ideas coming from this group.

To me, any change and focus of the organization should have an eclectic approach but in a single direction.'

Khan commented 'You are sounding like an Oxymoron Pabloo'. There was a burst of mild laughter from the group hearing the comment of Khan.

'You are sounding like an Oxymoron Pabloo'

'I am saying our ideas can come from diverse perspectives but the strategy as such should cover all aspects and which is long term and beneficial.'

Singh added, 'so Pabloo, how can we put all these together?' Pabloo added, 'all of it that was spoken here has one common thing. It is People, and they are the dynamic variable. If that has to be considered then we can use STEEPLE and CLIPS which is a[52] comprehensive approach.'

---

[52] Aguilar, F.J., (1967), Scanning the business Enviornment, 1st ed. New York, Macmillan company.

Singh asked, 'and how does it all get covered?' The group seemed to be curious as well.

Pabloo explained, 'STEEPLE is an acronym for Socio-cultural, Technological, Economic, Environmental, Political, Legal, and Ethical and CLIPS is an acronym for Culture, Layout, Innovation, Power, and Social components of the organization. If you observe, you will notice STEEPLE covers external aspects and CLIPS covers internal aspects. All our policies can be shaped considering all these aspects.'

Khan asked, 'it does cover almost all but how exactly it works? Can you throw us some light?'

'Sure' said Pabloo and added, 'let us take the Socio–cultural aspect. This is driven by demographic trends and population projections. The average age group of our company is 26, with 60:40% of male and female and with over 80% of them in the age group of 21 to 30 years, we can shape our policies with flexibility in our employee management policy including flexible hours and work from home or remote, clear careers paths, information kiosks, access to internets at secluded areas and mobile app-driven groups, all to keep the workforce motivated and engaged. To quote another one, Environmental, our CSR initiatives can include GO green initiatives such as moving towards a paperless office, saving electricity, and other range of philanthropic initiatives. Such initiatives will have profound involvement of employees because it brings purpose and value to them. With such initiatives, they feel connected to the organization that helps them to give back to society. This helps in both attracting and retaining employees. Likewise, we can debate each aspect in the context of our organization from external and internal standpoints. Many in the group seem to acknowledge this approach.

Shiva voiced out, 'I like this approach. It brings a methodology to the entire process.'

'Precisely, Shiva' said Pabloo and added, 'once we built on this, we will also notice a correlation between these aspects. To give you an example, the Technology aspect of STEEPLE can correlate to the Innovation aspect of CLIPS. Similarly, an Ethical aspect of STEEPLE can correlate with the Culture aspect of CLIPS.'

'Technology getting related to Innovation makes sense but how is Ethical connected to Culture? Khan asked.

Pabloo explained 'a good ethical practice and environment builds the right culture. Perhaps the underlying argument for ethical practices is that companies adopting them benefit by gaining employee commitment and loyalty to their workforce and improved organizational performance. This in turn builds a more trustful culture, a culture where the employees feel they are valued. These correlations can help us tremendously towards the desired outcome.'

'Got it' said Khan.

'I guess we all know now who is going to do some homework and come back to us with a presentation' said Singh jokingly. The whole group laughed aloud and mentioned 'Hear, hear!'

Pabloo joined the laughter and said, 'I guess, we will all spend some time individually and make this happen.'

Singh said, 'yes, I would like you to do it. You can present it in the deck that we are planning to have in the context of the new location.'

Pabloo nodded.

After lunch, there was a little bit of sightseeing before they boarded the bus. Around 5 PM, the bus reached Budapest and everyone was getting ready for the cruise ride. By 8 PM, they boarded the yacht for an hour-long cruise ride. Pabloo was excited like a teenager and took the first seat in the first row. As the yacht started, he took a deep breath enjoying the cold breeze and was mesmerized by the beauty. It was a beautiful ride. He had a panoramic view of the UNESCO World Heritage site such as the Buda Castle, Hungarian Parliament, Matthias Church, and Fisherman's Bastion and also the Gresham Palace, Hungarian Academy of Sciences, Historical bridges, and Churches, 19th-century Universities and Contemporary buildings. Truly it was an evening to remember for a lifetime. A real treat! As the yacht circled back after 45 minutes to the place it started, by the side of the river, he noticed the place where he met Michael. For some reason, he already missed meeting him today. He wished he planned the day in a way that he could have met him in the late evening. Michael has left a powerful & positive impression on him, especially through his eagerness to know things. Also, Michael reminds him of his father whom he lost when he was young. Pabloo all through his young years missed his father. He knows what it means not to have a father's love and guidance.

Dinner at the hotel was teamed up with wine and many other alcoholic beverages along with some fantastic food spreads. After some time, Pabloo headed back to the same sit-out area of the restaurant on the 10th floor and enjoyed the view and the breeze. He was feeling a little sad as the trip will end the next day. But at the same time, he was thankful to be part of this once-in-a-lifetime trip.

The Last Day

The last day was meant for shopping and anything that they wanted to do on their own. Pabloo did his bit for his family and friends and after a good lunch, he stepped out of the hotel to explore the local places all by himself. As he walked on the shopping alleys, he reflected on the European social market model. Also called Social democracy or Democratic socialism, it is built on a strong belief that the modern large corporation has important social effects and therefore needs to be brought more under democratic government control. Supporters of the social market economy also often desire to extend democratic government into areas such as work relations and education. They believe that a worker should have the same rights as a citizen does.

Another factor that they focus is on the egalitarian aspect. This does not require that everyone have the same income or wealth. But, it does require that "no one is richer or poorer than another that they cannot mix socially on equal terms". Supporters of the social market economy realize that some people will earn more than others. Further, they also believe that inequality should be sufficient to provide such incentives, but no greater. They believe that liberal market capitalist countries are subject to too many periodic recessions with all the difficulties that unemployment brings. The major parts of the liberal market capitalist economy are subject to a monopoly and also they believe that having all countries become liberal market capitalist economies would increase the disparities between the rich countries and the poor countries of the world. Supporters of the social market economy used to call themselves a Middle Way or a Third Way - a view of an economic system that is between liberal market capitalism and communism. He wondered how it will all have its implication from the HR standpoint. Maybe he should have it clarified with Rachel today evening. It will be rich learning from a fellow HR in a different continent. As he further strolled, he saw so many people from different walks of life. He just enjoyed this new experience!

Just after dinner around 8.30 PM, Pabloo headed towards the meeting spot. As he arrived he saw Michael and Rachel waiting for him. 'Hey, hello!' said Pabloo as he walked a little brisker towards them.

'Hey, Pabloo' said Rachel. Michael greeted him warmly, 'hello Pabloo, we missed you! How was your trip to Bratislava?'

'It was wonderful, Michael and I also missed you both' said Pabloo and added 'It saddens me; it is already the last day of my trip'. There was a comfortable and happy feeling the three of them experienced with each other's company.

Pabloo further added 'well Rachel, I wanted to ask you about the European social economic market'.

'Go ahead, Pabloo.'

'I am quite aware of the European social model but I'm curious about its implication in the labor market here and the Human Resources. Can you give me a general overview?'

Rachel started to explain, 'the first thing that comes to my mind is the unionization and the nature of collective bargaining. The labor union bargains for all workers in a company whether that worker is a member of the labor union or not. In principle, the labor union would want to increase the wages of all workers with other benefits such as work-life balance and therefore the employers undertake actions to make these workers more productive.'

Michael said, 'no wonder you have employees with grievances.'

Pabloo replied, 'well, it is definitely not something in Europe alone. You find such issues all over the world and the job of HR is always a challenging one given the management wants more production and the employees want more balance and leisure.'

Rachel continued, 'the other thing is, the representation of employees in the decision-making process through work councils.'

'Yes, I have read about it, it is called codetermination' mentioned Pabloo 'and by law in most European countries, one-third of the representatives on the Supervisory Board must be selected by the workers.'

Rachel added, 'generally there is good employment security for employees and there is a range of benefits.'

'Is it the same back in your country as well?' She asked further.

Pabloo said, it is a little different and I am wondering if there is any connection with different countries' work culture.'

Michael asked, '*do different countries have different working cultures?*'

'Yes, Michael' said Pabloo and continued, '*but before we get into that, let me clarify Rachel about her question. You see Rachel, just like the social market capitalist economies, we also have the liberal market capitalist economies. This is contrasting in a way because it sees the modern corporation as the private property of its owners and therefore the job is also the private property* of the employer. This means limited worker's rights, weak trade union organization, stronger right to manage; competitive labor markets, and larger wage differentials to name a few -all these present different kinds of HR implications and challenges such as attempts to increase cooperation from employees historically made difficult by conflictive industrial relations, more recently by low levels of employment security creating difficulties in obtaining commitment.'

'Both these economies sound very different.'

Pabloo answered, 'not exactly, Rachel. We should also note the important similarities. Both are basically capitalist economies, in that, most of the capital goods are privately owned. And in both systems, markets are of the greatest importance in allocating society's scarce resources. So the similarities among these types of economies are much greater than the differences.'

Michael asked, 'I am captivated to know about the different countries' work cultures.'

Pabloo answered 'then I have to mention Hofstede,[53] a Dutch social psychologist. He has done immense work around how working cultures in an organization can be different in different countries. He differentiated it through six dimensions, the last two dimensions were recently added, and the original four are Power distance - the degree of inequality that exists – and is accepted – between people with and without power. Individualism Versus Collectivism - the degree to which people in a society are integrated into groups. Masculinity Versus Femininity - refers to the distribution of roles between men and women. Uncertainty Avoidance Index - this dimension describes how well people can cope with anxiety. To give you an example Michael, between Hungary and India, India scores high in Power distance, and Hungary scores high in the other three dimensions.'

'Interesting!' said Michael.

Rachel asked, 'so, what is the connection that you were wondering, Pabloo?'

'I was thinking if there would be any pattern related to liberal and social economies to the work culture of a country in the Hofstede's dimensions we just spoke about.'

---

[53] Hofstede, G. (1991). Cultures and Organizations: Software of the Mind. London, UK: McGraw-Hill & Hofstede, G., Hofstede, G.J., Hofstede, M., (2010), "Cultures and Organizations, Software of the Mind", Third Revised Edition, McGraw-Hill.

Rachel asked 'and?'

'Such correlations, if not already done, can make an impact on the Human Resources aspect in the form of talent management and development. That is the beauty of HR, our ability to relate to many aspects given the complex structure of human behavior and business.'

Rachel expressed, 'Pabloo, I wanted to share something. All through yesterday and today, I'm feeling a lot more focused in the HR role that I am performing. I think a large part of it is because of the discussion that we had and of course, I love HR! But at the same time, am also self-doubting if I will be able to consistently express all those behaviors and qualities that are required for an HR professional. How can I make it consistent?'

Pabloo said, 'self-motivation is a technique you can employ to bring in this consistency and for which you need to know what motivates you. If you are looking for a concept or a framework, you might be interested to explore Enneagram[54] - a model of the human psyche which is principally understood and taught as a typology of nine interconnected personality types. Through this model, you can understand your personality type for a journey of self-understanding and self-development. Another tool you can consider using is MBTI[55]. Myers–Briggs Type Indicator - an introspective self-report questionnaire with the purpose of indicating differing psychological preferences in how people perceive the world around them and make decisions. There are many such tools and frameworks that are available for you to understand yourself and bring in that consistency. In my personal opinion, you should take an approach and accept that you will have hurdles and challenges in this journey and importantly this can only happen over a period of time.

---

[54] Riso, D.R., and Hudson, R., (1999) The Wisdom of the Enneagram: The Complete Guide to Psychological and Spiritual Growth for the Nine Personality Types, Bantam Books.

[55] Myers, I.B., (1998), MBTI Manual - A Guide to the Development and Use of the Myers-Briggs Type Indicator, Consulting Psychologists Press.

You should be brave enough to overcome your fear and inhibitions. For all of this to happen, you should start to believe in yourself. One way I reinstated this is through a goal sheet struck on the wall of my room.'

'Goal sheet?'

'Yes, Rachel. You need to write your goals like what you want to become and read them every day first thing in the morning. Meditation is another powerful way through which you can bring consistency.'

Michael asked almost immediately, 'how does meditation help?'

Pabloo answered, 'certain meditation techniques tremendously help increase the focus required to maintain consistency. Importantly you should enjoy this journey and not force yourself into it. If you really love what you wanted to become then there is a natural affiliation towards it.'

Both Michael and Rachel nodded in agreement.

Pabloo looked at his watch; it was over half an hour since they met. He further added, 'well, I guess I have to rush back to my hotel.'

'So soon? We just met.'

'Yes, Michael. I have an early morning 6 AM flight to catch.'

'Oh! I guess it is goodbye then' said Michael and further added, 'well, I got you this as a souvenir' and pulled out a painting by the side of his car seat.

'It is magnificent!' mentioned Pabloo. It was a charcoal sketch that resembled Pabloo with a background view of the river Danube capturing the picturesque Budapest ahead of it.

'Wow! How you got this painted?' asked Pabloo admiring the painting.

'I also have an artist in me' smiled Michael and added 'the conversations we had and the bond we have formed in such a short time has created a deep impact on me. This picture is my first sight of you and I painted it for you to remind you about our friendship by this riverside every time you look at it.'

'Thank you my friend!' said Pabloo smilingly.

Rachel smiled and said, 'I have not got you any gift, Pabloo'.

Pabloo smiled and said, 'the greatest gift you can give me is by being successful in the field of HR that you love the most, I wish you the very best in your efforts.'

Charcoal sketch that resembled Pabloo with a background view of the river Danube capturing the picturesque Budapest ahead of it.

Rachel smiled and said, 'thank you Pabloo. I am determined to make a difference as an upcoming HR!'

After some emotional moments, they bid goodbyes and parted ways with the hope to meet again.

Pabloo headed back to the hotel with a heavy heart on his last day in Europe. As he walked back he already started to think about the most important presentation coming up next week. He knows if he has to make a difference to his organization, his presentation should be strategic in nature and provide a high level of direction on the areas that have to be focused. He was wondering what element to bring in the presentation to explain his viewpoint to the leadership team and most importantly to make a difference!

Slide 1: Make No Mistake, Small is the New Big

'Thank you all for spending some time with me individually in the last month or so. Many of your ideas are well linked with the company's vision' mentioned Pabloo in the board room back in their Indian headquarters. 'I have prepared a deck by spending considerable time aligning it to our discussion with the company's goals.' Pabloo seemed to capture the interest of all the leaders. They seem excited about the session as a continuity of their last European discussion.

Pabloo clicked and the first slide appeared on the projector screen and it had one sentence alone with a creative, and the leaders seemed curious.

'Small is the new BIG'

Pabloo sounded confident and mentioned, 'we all agree that if our company has to compete in this period of economic globalization, open markets, hyper-competition and ever fast-changing environment, then we need to take fast decisions and act even faster upon the decisions made. This being the case, we need to learn to operate in small teams.'

'Are you saying the bigger is not better? I always thought many heads would bring in diversity and a range of ideas' quipped Shiva, the Sales head.

'Totally agree!' mentioned Pabloo almost immediately, 'but the only trouble is, along with it, it also brings Social Loafing'. Pabloo again noticed a bunch of curious faces that were intrigued to know about Social Loafing. He continued, 'Social Loafing'[56] curbs the efforts of making quick decisions and taking swift actions. Picture this: How many times have we all entered an all-important meeting and left the room without being able to make a decision? How often have we struggled to understand the project not being completed within the agreed timelines despite having a large team working on it? In both cases, the real culprit is what we thought throughout to be the differentiator - Bigger teams - and therefore, Social Loafing.'

'Interesting, Can you please add a few more insights, Pabloo?' asked Singh.

'Ask the Ringelmann[57] added Pabloo and continued, 'he would explain this through The Ringelmann effect - Individual members of a group tend to become less productive as the size of their group increases. It is true and I am sure every one of us would have noticed in our own

---

[56] Brickner, M. A., Harkins, S. G., & Ostrom, T. M. (1986). Effects of personal involvement: Thought-provoking implications for social loafing. Journal of Personality and Social Psychology,51(4), 763-769.

[57] Kerr, N.L., & Brunn, S.E.,(1981), Ringelmann Revisited: Alternative Explanations for the Social Loafing Effect, First Published, Research Article, https://doi. org/10.1177/014616728172007.

experiences. Typically, when the team size is big, participants tend to loaf more than they would have if they worked individually. It is because they realize there is no pressure for them to be at their best, given that they get away unnoticed even if their efforts are minimal. All of it works countercyclically to the original intent of the organization to put large teams in the first place and further the results only retrogrades!'

Singh smiled and commented, 'I need to count the number of people in this room', and a burst of mild laughter followed it. Pabloo was even more confident now, he further clicked on the laptop and the projector displayed more relevant information. He continued, 'Jeff Bezos, the founder and CEO of Amazon said it beautifully through his 'Two Pizza rule'[58] which means, if the team cannot be fed with two pizzas, then the team size is too big. The idea is that the more people you have working on the project, the more chaotic it can be, whereas smaller teams can make decisions faster and be in agreement. This is much needed given the pace of change organizations face and the need to be more agile than ever before. Gallup in its 2013 report called 'The state of the American workplace' found out the smallest companies have more engaged employees. This is a possible correlation of how large teams harbinger social loafing.'

Shiva raised a question, 'Does this mean, invariably, collaborating with larger teams will not yield the desired results?'

'No' retorted Pabloo, 'it just means it is much more powerful and effective with smaller teams given the need to cope with this rapid change and uncertainty. Put your trust in the research results published by CYBAEA through its popularly known 3/2 rule,[59] *which states 'if*

---

[58]   Giang, V. (2013). The 'two pizza rule' is Jeff Bezos' secret to productive meetings. Business Insider. Retrieved from www.businessinsider.com/jeff-bezos-two-pizza-rule-for-productive-meetings-2013-10.

[59]   Engelhardt, A. (2006): The 3/2 rule of employee productivity. CYBAEA Journal, http://www.cybaea.net/Blogs/Journal/employee_productivity.html (accessed: January, 2013).

you triple the number of employees you halve their productivity or when you increase the number of employees by 10%, then productivity falls by 6.3%' mentioned Pabloo.

This captured the interest of everyone, Singh asked a question, and 'how *do we go about setting this kind of an approach in an organization?'* We need to create a structure and an eco-system to support and develop such an organizational approach.'

'First, we need to promote an Intrapreneur mindset.[60] Have you noticed how successful entrepreneurs, one such as you, always collaborate with everyone to get ideas and recognize opportunities, albeit balance it with quick decision-making with risk-taking ability? Intrapreneurship is the concept of being an entrepreneur while working inside an organization. The critical advantage of promoting such a mindset is that it drives accountability and it is a natural game changer for any organization as accountability drives results. In simple words, responsibility and social loafing are bipolar. It is almost a CEO in the making. Just imagine the possibility of every project being driven by a CEO. The key here would be to be in consensus within the team or group and that is most effective when the team sizes are small.

Second, we need to recognize the efforts of the smaller teams and allow first-time mistakes: If you want results through smaller teams and Intreprenurship, then you must build a culture that allows them to experiment for results. It makes them creative, take risks and importantly be bold. They are no longer caught up in the hierarchy or high power distance and work towards results. Further, recognizing their efforts builds TRUST - a differentiator between winning and losing companies. Just look at successful companies and you will realize that they differ from what they were 3 to 5 years earlier. This is simply because they build trust with their people. Trust keeps social loafing at

---

[60] Pinchot, G., (1985) Intrapreneuring: Why You Don't Have to Leave the Corporation to Become an Entrepreneur, Harper & Row.

bay and a distinct advantage of a trust is its direct link to innovation and generally, such high trust workplaces embrace organizational change much more willingly.'

Khan, the Technology head quipped, 'Agreed about the smaller teams, but what about diversity then? How do we accommodate that factor? We all know diversity brings in rich results.'

Pabloo responded, *'the current workforce in our organization and even globally is the most multi-generational and diverse and therefore it is super important to bring in inclusivity – but in smaller pockets – in a way that it balances both a higher engagement resulting in higher productivity and therefore desired business results. It is of prime importance that we are faster in our decision and swifter in our actions, simply more agile!›*

Therefore to summarize...

- Firstly, develop Intrapranuer mindset
- Secondly, allow First-time mistakes
- And Thirdly, provide continuous coaching and mentoring

Singh seemed to be impressed and mentioned, 'Yes Pabloo, that seems to be the right thing to do.'

Slide 2: Technology and Innovation

'Technology is no longer an ambit of the advanced industries. It is available and open for all and has become essential in any value chain, thanks to its instantaneous two-way communication, easy accessibility, cheap cost, and global usability. In fact, it has become so common that they labeled generations such as Gen Y and Z after it. It is no longer the future. it is the present! Technology such as Automation, Digitization, AI, Telecommunication, etc. goes hand in hand with Innovation. Technology as an external factor is imported into the organization as Innovation. Technological innovation consists of the materials and processes used in organizational inputs to be converted into organizational output. And it goes without saying that we need to upgrade ourselves not only in Innovation but also in Disruptive Innovation.'[61]

Aarthi, the Quality head raised her eyebrow and asked 'are you saying we need to disrupt innovation? It seems to be contradictory. I was under the impression, we need to promote Innovation and not disrupt.'

'Allow me to explain this better' continued Pabloo, 'disruptive innovation does not mean we will stop promoting innovation; rather

---

[61] Christensen, C.M., (2016), The Clayton M. Christensen Reader, Harvard Business Review Press & Christensen, C.M.,Raynor, M.E., Gregersen, H., (2011) Disruptive Innovation: The Christensen Collection (The Innovator's Dilemma, The Innovator's Solution, The Innovator's DNA, and Harvard Business Review Article "How Will You Measure Your Life?"), Harvard Business Review Press.

we will drive innovation in all current processes with an intent to change it and create value.'

'Sounds tautological' quipped Aarthi.

'But at the same time, it is not' quickly responded Pabloo and continued, 'let me put it this way, all disruptive innovations are innovation but not all innovations are disruptive innovation.'

Aarthi's face had an expression demanding a better explanation.

'Innovation means making changes in something that is already established. For example, an existing process can be innovatively automated with the use of technology. On the other hand, disruptive innovation is a shift in how we think of our current way of operations to the consumers and bringing in radical change that can open up new markets and value networks. A good example of disruptive innovation is - how smartphones have disrupted laptops as the primary usage for people. Today, smartphone users have the same application, if not more, than laptop users and they have better accessibility and mobility when compared to the latter' explained Pabloo.

'Got it' mentioned Aarthi.

Pabloo continued, 'if we have to promote disruptive innovation then there is a need for us to have a mind shift to re-look at the way we are functioning and catering services to our clients and this is applicable across the board and not just for this group. We should also be mindful that disruptive innovation cannot happen overnight. However, with the right ecosystem we can bring this as part of our culture. This way, we continue to match the need for the speed of change through our existing innovative ways using technology, and at the same time, we will also put in efforts to re-look at the way we do business through disruptive thinking. At some level, these two meet and that will be the game changer.'

'Our primary focus should be allowing our talents to experiment for results in a way and a manner that your existing delivery will be business as usual. The experimentation for results should have a twofold objective. One is to increase and match the changing expectation of our clients, or in other words, innovate for a faster and quality delivery. The second would be to constantly relook at the entire engineering of doing things.'

'Wow, seems like a lot of work and may lead to some chaos the way we operate' mentioned the CEO Singh.

'If there is chaos then we are making progress, 'stated Pabloo confidently, ' Though I see where you are coming from. Let me say this: while we talk about Innovation, AI, Automation, Digitization, Disruption, etc., we should never forget that all of this comes from one source: Employees. We can truly make this happen if we engrain a talent mindset. A practical approach to such an organizational knowledge creation was created by Nonaka, an effective model to promote innovation combined with the legacy knowledge in the organization. It begins with sharing tactic knowledge through a SECI model.[62]

- Socialization – Tacit knowledge of individuals shared with others
- Externalization – Conversion of tactic knowledge into explicit metaphors, analogies, concepts, and models
- Combination – New knowledge is combined with existing knowledge
- Internalization – Whatever emerges from the combination is enacted and becomes a part of behavior and accepted

Another complimentary key initiative we need to take is to upskill our employees on the technological front: our organization has a multi-generational workforce. We need to specifically focus on training Gen X and Baby Boomers population on the technological front, as for Gen Y and Z, technology has been the way of life. And one effective way of doing this is through Reverse Mentoring.'

---

[62] Nonaka, I., Toyama, R. and Konno, N. (2000). 'SECI, Ba, and leadership: a unified model of dynamic knowledge creation'. Long Range Planning.

'Innovation became Disruptive Innovation and Mentoring is becoming Reverse Mentoring' chuckled Singh.

'You are right Chief, to raise the game we need to change from the very ground up' mentioned Pabloo. 'As a matter of fact, reverse mentoring brings twice the benefit of regular mentoring. Let me tell you why.

Firstly, it fosters a culture of continual learning for new perspectives and improved innovation. The only difference is now it is a two-way street. This, inturn, not only imparts the understanding of technological learning from the younger generation to the older but also becomes a platform to retain younger generation employees thanks to the job satisfaction they will derive from the program. Secondly, it will also reduce the generation gap between the employees with an improved knowledge transfer in both ways. Finally, of course, it is vital to design a framework for this reverse mentoring by establishing the purpose, identifying objectives and guidelines, making perfect matches through shared interests and values, and, importantly soliciting the participation of the protégés. All of these will be aligned with the final desired outcome of being a united workforce ready to accept the challenges that come along with the speed of change.

Another essential aspect that we need to focus on is that if we have to encourage innovation, this group should embrace leadership that promotes the same. Peter Drucker put it beautifully when he stated: "If you want something new, you have to stop doing something old." We need to constantly encourage our workforce to think and not be afraid to try something new. In many ways, it connects us to the previous slide of promoting Interprenual mindset, allowing first-time mistakes and continuous investment in upskilling the workforce, encouraging innovative Ideas but clarifying priorities.

Let's remember, many believe we are outpacing Moore's law[63] which states technological processing power will double every 18 months. Now, if we have to compete with that, then we need to be open to new ideas and be ready for change.'

'Agree! But to be specific, I am more curious to know how we prepare our workforce for change or for the speed of change in particular?' asked the sales head, Shiva.

'Sure Shiva, it is explained in the upcoming slide' mentioned Pabloo.

---

[63] Moore, E.G., & Moore, E.G., "Cramming More Components Onto Integrated Circuits", Electronics Magazine, vol. 38, no. 8, pp. 114-117, April 1965.

Slide 3: Change and the Speed of Change

'The world is changing faster than ever' mentioned Pabloo as he clicked to the next slide. 'A lot of us will agree that change is the only constant, but we need to be mindful of the speed of change. Until about 5 years ago, the focus was that the companies should be adaptable and open to change. But now, it is a norm, in fact, a basic hygiene factor. Given this, if we have to differentiate ourselves from the rest, then the speed of change will determine the winning companies. You all must have heard the story of placing grains on the chessboard squares. If you were to start with a single grain of rice, then put two grains on the second square, four grains on the next, and so on until the 64th and final square, you would end up with a mountain of rice that would tower over Mount Everest. The amount will be 1,000x in the present-day global production of rice. Google director of Engineer, Ray came up with the concept of the second half of the chessboard.[64] The idea basically is that when the rice begins to reach the second half of the chessboard, growth becomes exponential. Gentlemen, today we are in the second half of the chess board, we need to prepare to accept the unprecedented amount of change naturally, and as they say, 'Change is like a totem before which we prostrate and in the face of which we are powerless'.[65]

---

[64] Kurzweil, R., (2000), The Age of Spiritual Machines - When Computers Exceed Human Intelligence, Penguin Publishing Group.

[65] Grey, C. (2005) A very short, fairly interesting and reasonable cheap book about studying organizations, Sage: London.

This brings us to the vital question, how do we prepare to embrace change as an organization?

Here are my three main takes:

First, before we consider changes, we need to anticipate resistance to change and design a coping and support mechanism. Research cites[66] three primary reasons for resistance to change in organizations. Firstly, the logic of management actions and behaviors is sometimes obscure. Secondly, if a change occurs, the accumulated intellectual experience of the players becomes devalued and change is taken as a personal threat (so a safety net is needed). Thirdly, employees need to have their hands held while they are learning. This being the case, we need to ensure people who will face change are prepared to see its benefits. One scholar[67] suggested an effective 4 practical ways to overcome resistance.

Benefit: Employees should see the benefit of change. In other words, the change should have a clear relative advantage for the individuals being asked to change; it should be perceived as a better way.

Compatibility: The change should be as compatible as possible with the existing values and experiences of the people being asked to change.

Complexity: The change should be no more complex than necessary. It must be as easy as possible to understand and use.

Trialability: The change should be something that people can try on a step-by-step basis and make adjustments throughout the process.

If you sum all the above four, we will know at some level, it requires us to educate and train our employees continuously in both the technical

---

[66] Allio, R. J. (2008a). C. K. Prahalad heralds a new era of innovation. Strategy & Leadership, 36(6),11-14. doi: 10.1108/10878570810918304.

[67] Coch, L., & French, J. R. P., Jr. (1948). Overcoming resistance to change. Human Relations, 1, 512–532. https://doi.org/10.1177/001872674800100408.

and the non-technical aspects. This brings up the complimentary second point.

Second, be a learning organization. For it to happen, we need to make an organizational effort that promotes learning as a way of living. There are many frameworks that provide direction to an organization that wishes to progress in this learning journey. In Particular,[68] Crossan suggests a model of organizational learning (OL) involving four processes of creating and applying knowledge. Their '4-Is model' involves:

- Intuiting – Individuals explain and see patterns in their experience which provide new insights
- Interpreting – Individuals explain insights to themselves and then to others
- Integrating – The group shares in the understanding and takes action
- Institutionalizing – The learning at individual and group levels becomes organizational through systems, structures, procedures, and strategy

'Third, we need to Tango with T&C' said Pabloo.

Singh commented, 'building a dancing floor, eh?' mild laughter followed but Pabloo sensed a need to emphasize the importance of T&C Tango.

Pabloo responded smilingly, 'yes, we always need to bring joy to our office environment. But here, T&C stands for Trust and Change. I purposefully added the Tango element as these two elements need to be gracious in their relationship in an organizational context. I could not emphasize more on the importance of Trust. It is a panacea to all our organizational challenges. So let me dwell a little on Trust.

Trust – It is defined as a psychological state comprising the intention to accept vulnerability based upon positive expectations of the intentions

---

[68] M. Crossan, H.W. Lane, R.E. White, An organizational learning framework: From intuition to institution, Academy of Management Review, 24 (1999), pp. 522-537.

or behavior of another.'[69] so, is this about willingness to make oneself vulnerable in the face of uncertainty or insecurity? Or is that risk-taking ability? The word Trust can be very different between being trustworthy and trusting others. Being trustworthy, to a large extent, can be justified and rationalized as it is mostly internal, within oneself, and it takes the expression of Ability, Benevolence, Integrity, Predictability, etc. It is the latter, trusting others, which comes to play through the social process that can be tricky because there are too many variables and uncertainties. In an organizational context, it becomes even more complex as we are dealing with Trust between individuals and between individuals and management. That being said, there are ways to build Trust in this dynamic and ever-changing environment.'

For T&C to Tango, the Past, Present and Future should be considered in organizations.

Past, though it is unusual to consider the past, it is essential to curb a particular organizational virus behavior called Cynicism. Usually displayed by a bunch of people, Cynics differ from people who resist change in a way that they neither resist nor tend to be enthused about change. Both can be contagious in the form of apathy, disengagement, and lack of enthusiasm leading to organizational cancer if not diagnosed. One way of overcoming this would be to promote consistent organizational management and leadership characteristics of Benevolence and Integrity. A great deal of that would be related to the avoidance of Pseudo consultation and promoting a genuine interest involving employees. It is important not to mislead people into thinking that things will be better or more successful than they are. Under-promising and over-delivering tend to work better than over-promising and under-delivering.

Present, through the level of Psychological contracting. Simply put, it concerns employees' subjective beliefs, shaped by the organization,

---

[69] Rousseau, D.M., S. Sitkin, R.S. Burt and C. Camerer (1998), 'Not so different after all: A cross-discipline view of trust', Academy of Management Review, 23, 393–404.

about its current role as an employer. This is a crucial factor for organizations that embrace changes through high trust. For it to be successful, we should understand that both parties can have different belief systems. Therefore success is the concept of mutuality. This can be achieved by Balanced and Relational psychological contracting. Key features of such contracting would be open-ended and relationship-oriented employment with well-specified performance terms subject to change over time. Openness, Transparency, and Communication are some of the critical ingredients of mutual expectations with an overall interest in the employee-employer relationship.

Future, it is directly linked with T&C and People quoted 'Change is ultimately about people – if they do not change, nothing significant happens'. People resist change because of a multitude of factors in organizations. The best way to address this would be through Change agents. Their key responsibility should be to ensure that the people affected by change know how it satisfies criteria such as Benefit, Compatibility, and Complexity, the parameters we glanced through earlier. One effective way to do this would be to identify the resistors and give them the responsibility of being a Change agent. The advantage of such an approach is twofold. First, People tend to support change initiatives that they are part of. Second, their conviction about change can be so powerful, given that they have experienced resistance in the past. This can promote a culture of High Trust and Change across the organization.

If we build this platform, T&C Tango will generate thundering applause, given the complexities of its moves. But we need to be mindful of the number of interacting elements that can behave in a non-linear fashion. Almost all through the performance, the success lies in complementing the moves between the partners of T&C, the music, and the stage. So, while it will not always be possible to score a perfect ten, it will be possible to set the ball rolling toward it. Now Singh, will you sponsor building this dancing floor?' asked Pabloo with a grin.

'Yes'! Singh answered firmly.

'Thank you Singh' Pabloo followed and added, 'Now these will equip us to handle change but for us to be more agile for the speed of change, we need one more dancing couple and that is M&C!'

Slide 4: Motivation and Communication

' *A*s I mentioned earlier', continued Pabloo, 'If we truly want our workforce to not just change but transform, then, we got to exercise OCB.[70]

'Some sort of Martial Law?' said Krish with a gentle smile. Krish, the Finance head, is known for his sense of humor and for speaking his mind out.

Pabloo continued, 'Indeed, we all agree on one thing. Any effective change is only possible if the change comes within. We cannot coerce or force them, even so, we may get some initial results but it will never be sustainable. And to answer your query Krish, OCB is not force-fed on employees. OCB stands for Organizational Citizenship Behavior. OCB is the discretionary effort people could give if they wanted to, but above and beyond the minimum required. As leaders, we should focus on understanding why any employee would like to increase discretionary efforts. It is not rocket science; we just have to be genuine in our approach to the concerns of our employees. Studies suggest many approaches to this outcome. One particular approach[71] can be by driving the four engagement parameters.

---

[70] Bateman, T.S., & Organ, D.W., (1983), Job satisfaction and the good solider: The relationship between affect and employee "citizenship". Academy of Management Journal, 26, 587-595.

[71] Holbeche,L.S., Matthews,G., (2012), Engaged: unleashing the potential of your organisation through employee engagement, John Wiley/Jossey Bass.

- Connection: Employees need a sense of identification and pride working in an organization. There has to be a common purpose and value
- Voice: Managers need to keep employees informed about the organizational progress and change and listen to employees' views for them to be involved
- Support: Employees need to be felt valued and be treated fair, they should believe their employer is concerned with their well being
- Scope: Work should be purposeful with meaning, there should be an opportunity for growth and allow autonomy underpinned by mutual trust

'Where is motivation in this?' asked Krish.

'I am getting there Krish' responded Pabloo. 'If we have to drive the above, then motivation should never be seen as something to apply. It should be an inbuilt ingredient and a hygiene factor to manage and develop people. There are many approaches to motivation, but on the whole, motivation can be content-oriented or process-oriented. Content-oriented focus on rewards and outcomes that motivate people, but the process takes an approach to how people are motivated cognitively. An approach that I find appealing that can be suited to an organization like ours would be a process motivation driven by a formula'.

$$F = E * I * V$$

'Developed by Vroom as an Expectancy theory,[72] this motivation approach gives an analytical approach and strikes a balance between Intrinsic and Extrinsic motivation. It states Individuals are motivated to increase performance through the formula above. Here,

---

[72] Vroom, V.H., & Deci, E.L., (1972), Management and Motivation - Selected Readings, Penguin Education.

- **F** *is the force of motivation, i.e. how much effort will be applied ('how hard I am willing to work').*
- **E** *is expectancy, i.e. the belief that extra effort will result in better performance ('if I work harder, my output will increase')*
- **I** *is instrumentality, i.e. the belief that better performance will lead to a reward ('if my output increases, I will get a reward').*
- **V** *is valence, the perceived value of the reward ('how much I want the reward').* Valence links back to content theories of motivation, which tell us that individuals are motivated by many factors (needs and wants), including money, security, affiliation, power, achievement, status, growth, and more.

All our rewards and recognition programs should be aligned with this analytical approach. Together we can establish SMART goals that are Specific, Measurable, Achievable, Realistic, and Time-bound. We should also be mindful of striking a balance between motivation and performance. This is because today's motivation for rewards and recognition will become tomorrow's norm, and employees may no longer appreciate the norms' explained Pabloo.

'So you are saying we need to keep increasing the rewards programs? And if that is the case, where do we draw the line as all of these are expenses or costs' asked Krish.

Pabloo responded, 'I am saying we should have a clear distinction between Extrinsic and Intrinsic motivation and balance between these two for a motivated performance. And Krish, coming to your point, Extrinsic is more tangible and Intrinsic is more internal. Therefore motivation does not always mean cost or expense to the company. There are studies to show money can reduce motivation.'

'Well, Pabloo, I would like to hear more on that' mentioned Krish.

Pabloo continued, 'Given that money is a motivator, it should be noted it is not the primary driver. Evidence suggests money can reduce the effectiveness of intrinsic motivation and there are circumstances when it appears to. The deciding factor in most cases is not what is done but how it is done. Even if money is a primary motivational factor, employees compare their rewards with colleagues and if they perceive unfair treatment, they are motivated to act in a way that affects their performance. Also, money does not make people feel unique. Therefore, as I mentioned earlier, we should strike a balance and focus more on emotional drivers. A scholar recommended one such approach,[73] which has four primary drivers that underpin every motivated act. They are:

- The drive to acquire - Mainly physical goods, like money, enhances our social status and allows us to compare ourselves to others
- The drive to bond – People need to have a positive emotional bond with their organization and the people within
- The drive to comprehend – Seeking meaning and contribution, seeking challenges and the scope to learn and grow
- The drive to defend – By promoting justice and feelings of security, as well as the need to maintain the status quo

'Agree, in fact, I'm able to relate my own career through these drivers' mentioned Krish.

'Thank you, Krish. Through this balanced approach, we will not only be an agile workforce to embrace change but also be flexible and motivated to match the pace of change. But to make all of these happen, we need to consider one component which cuts across the organization in all our efforts, and that is communication. Communication is the foundation of any successful organization. It should build upon the pillars of Transparency, Positive Reinforcement, and Relationship Management. Developing others, fostering teamwork and total collaboration creating synergies between people will also help. Before we dwell on it, let

---

[73] Nohria, N., & Groysberg, B., (2008), Employee Motivation: A powerful new model, Harvard Business Review 86(7-8):78-84, 160

us get one thing straight. Communication is not always explicit. We also communicate when we do not communicate! Before I invite any questions or comments on this, let me explain this. Most, if not all the time, it is not only about what and how we communicate but also what we are not communicating and what message we are sending by not communicating. A classic example is when management fails to communicate about the organization's health. It needs to constantly communicate how it is growing or facing challenges in a trusted and confident manner. By sheer transparent communication, the organization can avoid speculation about its present and future and earn the respect of its employees. Similarly, all of its processes, systems, and even office designs should aim to strengthen communication.'

'Designs? How does it fall in this?' asked Singh curiously.

'Glad you asked that question Singh' continued Pabloo. 'You see, a working paper 'The good, the bad and the productive'[74] published some interesting data, it stated a symbiotic pairing of workers in physical space can improve communication and in turn performance by some 15%. If we go by that, then the workplace should be designed in a manner that can have closer proximity of the two workers. This calls for a creative way of designing the workstations as pairing cubicles. Contribution can go beyond identifying which types of workers should be paired together, and how we can create symbiotic relationships by pairing those with opposite strengths for synergy.

Another aspect of the workstation's design is providing a range for an employee to reach out to a manager. Though this is an age of technology, in-person human interaction has its own merit. The workstations can be designed in such a way; any employee can reach their manager in the shortest range physically possible. Communication can be super improved through creative designs involving a circular arrangement of

---

[74] Michael,H., & Minor,D., (2016), "Workplace Design: The Good, the Bad, and the Productive." Harvard Business School Working Paper, No. 16-147.

workstations so that the pairing cubicles and the manager's cubicles are part of a circle. Simply put, any employee should be able to view his fellow team members and manager in a single frame of his vision. Such circular arrangements with well-designed desks are linked to positive emotions which aid creativity and productivity. These in turn promote the development of a collective mindset bringing teams closer together.'

'Interesting' mentioned Singh.

'Absolutely, like I said, communication is a two-way street and it does not always have to be explicit. That being said let me tell you one important area where we can improve explicit communication. Feedback is one of the most granted words taken in the corporate world. Almost all of us are always eager to give feedback to another person, but least concerned about the other person while pointing out their weakness.

Shiva intervened, 'hold on, is there something wrong in giving feedback? It is the responsibility of a manager to give feedback and what could possibly be wrong with that?'

Pabloo replied firmly, 'feedback is absolutely necessary but the way we give feedback is what we need to take into consideration. Know this, on average, there are 13 criticism in a feedback mechanism by managers during appraisal.[75] Many researches state that in 33% of cases, performance was negatively affected.[76] We may still argue that we must tell our subordinates what we must say and we e cannot place it on a platter, especially when we are dealing with tight deadlines and that in a corporate world happens every time! But the fact of the matter is if the purpose of feedback is to improve performance, then we are working towards it countercyclically. This brings us to the critical point of how feedback should be given.

---

[75] Meyer, H.H., Kay, E., & French, J.R.P., (1965), Split roles in performance appraisal. Harvard Business Review, 43 (1), 129-142.

[76] DeNesi, A.S., & Kluger, A., (2000), Feedback effectiveness: Can 360-degree appraisals be improved? Academy of Management Perspectives 14(1):129-139.

Members who are giving feedback should be trained in the concepts of emotional intelligence and coaching. They should be made aware of the impact that they can have on individuals. There are effective ways to drive such performance communication through Behavior Anchored Rating Scales (BARS)[77] – which describe effective and ineffective performance. Behavioral Observation Scales (BOS)[78] – which are observable, job-related behaviors. It is also equally important to train the person who gets the feedback. A good way would be to coach them to become Feedback seekers[79] through learning-goal orientation – the willingness of managers to develop new skills and master new situations. All of these contribute an effective two-way communication. By preparing your workforce, you are making them embrace change and be equipped for the rate of change. As someone quoted, management is the process of communicating, coordinating and accomplishing actions in the pursuit of organizational goals, while maintaining relationships at work.'[80]

'Aim for a good change!' mentioned Singh.

Pabloo responded, 'Just a correction there Singh, we should not aim for change, we should aim for transformation and that is possible only with the right leadership!'

---

[77] Toquam, L, J., (1988), Development and Field Test of Behaviorally Anchored Rating Scales for Nine MOS, U.S. Army Research Institute for the Behavioral and Social Sciences, University of Minnesota.

[78] Latham, P.G., & Wexley, N.K., (1977), Behavioral Observation Scales for Performance Appraisal Purposes, Wiley Online Library, Citations: 123.

[79] VandeWalle, D., & Cummings, L. L. (1997). A test of the influence of goal orientation on the feedback-seeking process. Journal of Applied Psychology, 82(3), 390–400.

[80] Clegg, S.R., Kornberger, M., Pitsis, T., (2011), Managing and Organizations - An Introduction to Theory and Practice, SAGE Publications.

Slide 5: Leadership

'What is leadership?' asked Pabloo and continued, 'a search in Google with the keyword 'leadership' throws up 500 million results in less than a fraction of a second. It is huge and vast, according to one report; we spend 14 billion dollars a year on leadership development. No kidding![81] The term 'Leadership' invokes so much debate, opinions, and judgment even so much, that we have polls around it. But essentially, we need to understand the difference between Leader and Leadership.'

'Leadership is an extension of being a Leader' quipped Shiva.

'Thanks, Shiva let me explain this a little better. The basic distinction between Leader and Leadership is - the earlier can be a successful individual who exhibits a particular influence among others and achieve team goals, but the latter, added to the earlier, is different in a way it also recognizes the importance and the success of the followers. At the heart of leadership are qualities such as being ethical, high integrity, and benevolence that sets them apart. I have to tell you this, I have studied extensively about Leadership from many successful people and authors but the most appealing Leadership lesson I learned was from my nine-year-old niece!

---

[81] Johnson, W.M., & Suskewicz, J., (2020), Lead from the Future - How to Turn Visionary Thinking Into Breakthrough Growth, Harvard Business Review Press. O'Leonard, K., & Krider, J., (2014), Leadership development facebook 2014: Benchmarks and trends in U.S Leadership development, Bersin by Deloitte.

'Nine-year-old? Really, wow!' exclaimed Singh.

'Yes, 9-year-old!' continued Pabloo, 'I need to elaborate on this. She is a candidate for this subject, a junior people Leader in her school; I did ask her if she believed that she has served in her best capacity as a Leader. She nonchalantly responded, 'YES'! Taking an interest, I further asked, what makes her think that way and how would she articulate the top three qualities or attributes. She thought for a few seconds and mentioned - first, being kind and caring for the group. Second, taking responsibility for the group's actions and third being independent and strong, with an ability to look at options. I was just blown away for a minute there listening to her. In all my professional life, I have not come across anyone who is so confident and spontaneous in answering questions about leadership. After a pause, I asked her again 'how did she know what she mentioned was true.'

She retorted, 'I have been reading and observing so many people and importantly I performed the role and that is how I know what it takes!'

'Her answer spontaneously moved me. It touched my heart; a nine-year-old deeply understood leadership by the meaning of social relationships in her world. But, I continued, 'then who, according to you, are the best leaders if you have to name a few?'

'Gandhiji, my class teacher and most importantly my father' she answered.

'I was shocked again. In today's time, adults quote names such as the Bill Gates and Steve Jobs of the world, here is a nine-year-old quoting 2 out of 3 names through real-time experience.'

She continued, 'see, the way I see it, Leader is not about self but everything about others. It is those qualities that will help us to be successful!'

'So there you go, that is a Leadership lesson from a nine-year-old!' mentioned Pabloo and continued 'If you reflect upon the answers given by her, you will be able to make sense, get meaning, purpose and a direction toward Leadership:

First, being kind and caring for the group - This genuine quality of going beyond self-interest towards the interest of others is an essential attribute of a leader. Throughout history and the present, successful leaders exhibited compassion and empathy towards individuals and societies with high integrity and honesty at the core of it. This quality set them aside as a leader and brought them success through their journey, even when they were not recognized formally as a leader. Robin Sharma captured this beautifully in his book 'The leader who had no titles'. He stated that to be a great leader, first become a great person. For me, greatness starts when you become genuinely concerned about the welfare of others. Perhaps, when we relentlessly work towards the well-being of others, our meaning for success goes beyond extrinsic motivation such as titles, money, and possessions and sees oneness among everyone and everything that we do as a way of higher being. Then, the energies unleash for greatness within and around, and people look up to you as a leader.

Second, taking responsibility for the group's action - Our honorable late president Dr. Abdul Kalam once shared an experience in his book -Wings of Fire, which seems very apt in this context. The year was 1979, and after ten years of hard work, India was on the verge of launching its first-ever experimental rocket 'Roshini Technology Payload'. The project was driven under the leadership of Prof. Satish Dhawan and Dr.Abdul Kalam played a key role under him. The whole of the nation was looking forward to the success of the launch. But, unfortunately, the launch was a failure and the rocket plunged into the deep waters of the Bay of Bengal. Dr.Abdul Kalam was pointed out as one of the reasons for the failure. Dejected and concerned about the criticism, Dr.Abdul Kalam was unsure how to face the media. At that time, Prof. Satish faced the media, took the blame upon himself, and promised they would be successful next time. Exactly a year from then, Dr.Kalam and the team were able to make a successful launch, and the whole world praised them. There was jubilation across the country, and at the time of the public press conference, Prof. Satish Dhawan gave credit to Dr.Abdul Kalam and made him address the media! This sums it up as what is meant by taking responsibility for a group's actions. You can use many adjectives such as inspiration, empowerment, trust, etc., but most importantly, it is the willingness to own the team!

Third, independent and strong, with an ability to look at options - A well-respected Sadhguru once said, 'A leader is someone who can see things which others are not able to see'. This is just too true and this gets developed only through a strong sense of awareness and commitment which makes them strong and emotionally balanced with an ability to look at options and make the right decisions. It is the sense of responsibility that develops this commitment. There has to be a conscious effort to build this commitment and the first two points of caring and taking responsibility for the team forms the foundation for this ability. A critical aspect of this ability would be to build awareness among oneself. Importantly, this awareness should be built on experience and not entirely academic. Building awareness presently in our experience is the root strength of leadership. As the famous Sadhguru said, if you become aware, new possibilities open up and you elevate yourself to a higher level.'

'All of these sound great to hear Pabloo but how do we bring it into practice? asked Shiva.

'We need to 'Walk the Talk' through Servant Leadership!'[82] Pabloo mentioned confidently. 'You see the power of servant leadership is such that its focus is entirely upon the followers. It positions the

---

[82] Greenleaf, R. K., Frick, D.M., & Spears, L.C., (1996) On Becoming a Servant Leader - The Private Writings of Robert K. Greenleaf, Wiley.

leader as a steward than a commander with a commitment to serve the organization than personal ambition. The key attributes we all need to practice servant leadership will include humility, authenticity, empathy, and a willingness to put the needs of others above those of the self when providing direction.'

'Agreed' said Shiva and continued, 'but then again if you look at it, there are so many driving factors that shape the leader's behavior. Most of the time, the situation does not favor a leader to exhibit the qualities. What good can come from the attributes if the people around them do not appreciate them? Worst, what if such attributes are perceived as weak leadership?'

'You are right' Pabloo continued, 'Our biggest problem in the adult world is we tend to over-attribute the success or failure of situations to individual leaders. Known as a concept of Romance of Leadership[83] we tend to ignore contextual factors such as environment and followers. We either glorify or degrade the leaders based on the outcome. But this is exactly where a servant leader will stand tall. If you look at the attributes of a servant leader, it has everything to do with others and nothing to do with the self. When this is practiced genuinely, any hurdles that come in the path of a servant leader will only become a stepping stone for the leader to exhibit the qualities even more intensely. Let's face it, Leadership is not for everyone! But if the leaders in this room mindfully practice this in everyday of life through awareness, then we can make a world of difference!

Bottom line - To be a LEADER, FIRST BE A SERVANT!'

---

[83] Peterson, L., & Felfe, J., (2007), Romance of Leadership and management decision making, European Journal of Work and Organizational Psychology, 16:1, 1-24, https://doi.org/10.1080/13594320600873076.

'So true Pabloo, but it still does not answer my question entirely' mentioned Shiva. 'I mean, how do we tie all of these together in the context of our organization? How do we move from Good to Great?

Pabloo answered almost instantaneously, 'through our people practices and that is my next slide.'

Slide 6: People Practices

'RBVF!' echoed Pabloo's voice in a firm tone. He said, 'before anyone becomes curious, RBVF stands for Resource Based View of the Firm.[84] The significance of RBVF is so much that it led to a change from an 'outside-in' approach to an 'inside-out' approach in people strategy. RBVF states every organization has a unique bundle of assets, including human assets, and access to these and the ability to make effective use of them gives them a competitive advantage. Therefore, the key aspect of this is to develop the internal human capital, not just the behavioral aspect but also the skills, knowledge, and ability.

This is important because every individual in the organization would have developed a specific peak performance with the organization. We need to leverage the expertise of those individuals for us to stay competitive and sustainable. The key here is to identify if the resources are Valuable, Rare, Inimitable, and Non-substitutable. (VRIN)[85] we need to look at our organization's talent pool, identify such resources and map them to a matrix of Performance VS Potential. General Electric's nine-box Talent model will come in handy for this exercise.[86]

---

[84] Barney, J. (1991) Firm Resources and Sustained Competitive Advantage. Journal of Management, 17, 99-120.

[85] Barney,J. (1995). Looking Inside for Competitive Advantage. Academy of Management Executive, 9(4), pp. 49-61.

[86] Gay, M., & Sims, D., (2007) Building Tomorrow's Talent: A Practitioner's Guide to Talent Management and Sucession Planning, Author House.

Performance VS Potential

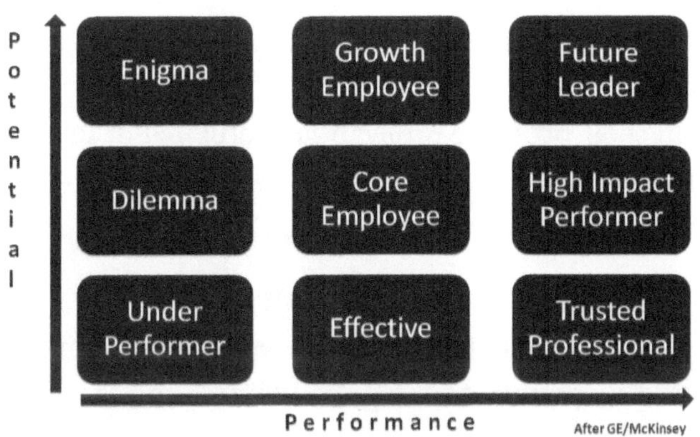

Once we have done this categorization, we need to identify a road map for each of these boxes marrying RBVF. The box on the top right will justify VRIN. However, our purpose of this talent development activity should also revolve around the factor of moving the boxes adjacent to the top right to the top right itself. Through this talent journey, we will also unleash the potential of the individuals for a win-win gain. Our primary focus should be on individuals who may fall under the box closer to the top right. They may be a few tabs lesser in performance or potential, but we can unleash their peak performance with specific skill-based training and coaching/mentoring. Care must be taken that our talent practices do not fall prey to 'Peter's Principle'.

'Who is Peter? And why is he coming here?' quipped Singh.

Pabloo continued passionately, 'The Peter principle[87] is a concept in management theory formulated by educator Laurence J. Peter and published in 1969. It states that the selection of a candidate for a position is based on the candidate's performance in their current role, rather than on abilities relevant to the intended role. Thus, employees

---

[87]   Peter, J.L., & Hull, R., (1969) The Peter Principal, Harper Collins.

only stop being promoted once they can no longer perform effectively, and "managers rise to the level of their incompetence".'

Simply put, individuals in a hierarchy get promoted to the next level based on their performance in their current role. This promotion continues until they reach a level where they are no longer competent to perform in their promoted role and eventually put into staying in it. The more significant point is that they remain at this level, above the last level at which they were competent. Consequences include:

The individual's incompetence in performing their elevated leadership role limits organizational growth. And there is more to it; we also lose a competent individual from the previous role, and there is a threat of another incompetent individual filling it. Not to mention a whole toxic culture that can get built under and around the Leader (subordinates, peers, etc.) in the form of defense, including Leathery, Cynicism and Office Politics

Importantly, the human capital management objectives of innovation and development of individuals, teams, and group hits a roadblock as learning stops

On analysis, this can prove to be a major handicap for organizations. We might argue that the premise is somewhat overstated as it is the natural way individuals and organizations evolve. With the right training, we can mold individuals to be successful in their roles. But the fact is, despite our effective succession planning and training intervention, there are always incompetent bosses and individuals who continue to prove Peter's principle right!

There was a range of suggestions and recommendations, including Adequate Skill Training, Effective Succession Planning, Demotion, etc. All these are effective ways, albeit only sometimes good enough. We require more options considering the complexity of expectations that arises with an elevated role.

Some of the organizational practices we can include in overcoming Peter's principle would be:

First,

To start with, we would need to introduce one-year promotion (4 quarters) to prepare individuals, especially for the roles of middle and senior management leaders. In the first quarter, not precisely an internal job moonlighting, but individuals are expected to engage 4 working days in their competent current role and one working day in their future role that they are going to get elevated to. Similarly for the next 3 quarters, there can be a decrease in the number of working days in a week for the current role and a subsequent increase in the working days for the future role until a full-fledged transition happens for the new role by the end of the 4th quarter.

The rationale behind such an approach is through the proven blended learning concept of 70:20:10,[88] which states 70% of the time we learn through our experience and challenging assignments, 20% through social learning, and 10% through theoretical framework. Through the one-year promotion plan, opportunities are created for the individual to experience real-time challenging work, learn through social relationships, and regular coursework and training in the form of workshops. Such an approach will increase an individual's learning and discretionary effort for a higher commitment and focus toward a future role. In parallel, the organization also establishes a TRUST level of believing/investing in the individual with balanced and relational psychological contracting.

Progress review can happen at the end of each quarter and all possible developmental support including 360-degree feedback can be provided

---

[88] Jennings, C., (2013), 70:20:10 Framework Explained, Creating High Performance Cultures, Forum Pty Limited, Center for Creative Leadership. (n.d.), The 70-20-10 rule of leadership development. Retrieved https://www.ccl.org/articles/leading-effectively-articles/70-20-10-rule/.

for the individuals. Based on the outcomes of every quarter, individuals within the organization can even opt out of the program, given that there is continuity between the current and future roles.

Second,

Harvard Business Review had responded in the "The Real Peter Principle: Promotion to Pain,"[89] arguing that what happens is that managers are promoted, not to their level of immutable incompetence, but to their level of anxiety and depression, which overwhelms their ambition and desire to succeed. If we go anything by that, then we need to ensure the right psychological balance and support are provided for the individuals who have been identified as having high potential. In the big five personality attributes[90] needed for leadership including openness, conscientiousness, extraversion, agreeableness, and neuroticism, emotional stability (Neuroticism) comes the closest to mediate and moderate the levels of anxiety and depression. Michael Goleman in his book Emotional Intelligence[91] proved how neuroticism can be used in the form of self-awareness, social awareness, self-management, and relationship management to overcome anxiety, depression, and anger.

The good news is recent trends in the world of management training and developments reflect renewed attention to the highly personal nature of leadership, in particular strategic leadership. In addition, current trends find emotional intelligence as a relevant and learnable leadership skill, intrinsic to the satisfactory execution of leadership.

---

[89] The real Peter Principle: promotion to pain. Harvard Business Review - Hess, H. H. (1976).

[90] John, E.F., Schuerger, J.M., & Watterson, D.G., (1980), Personality measures as predictors of managerial performance and salaries. Paper presented at the meeting of the Midwest Soceity for Multivariate Experimental Psychology, St. Louis, MO.

[91] Goleman, D., (2006), Emotional Intelligence - Why It Can Matter More Than IQ. Random House Publishing Group.

So in simple words, emotional intelligence is MUST and this should not only be restricted to the high echelons but also for all the employees at the beginning of their career developmental journey.

Third,

Most often, individuals push themselves for promotion because of peer pressure and to prove a point that they are not lesser than anyone else being considered for the role. There is almost always a perception that those who do not get promoted are incompetent. This has to change and HR has a role to play in this. The point has to be communicated effectively through its grades and bands, policies and system, rules and social components of the organization.

Again, this initiative calls for creative and innovative policies. One such policy can be: two or three promotions over a specific band should earn an employee all the benefits and perks and, importantly the status of being recognized as a value creator irrespective of the promotions. This way, they are not pressurized or motivated extrinsically in the long run. The key here would be to build an organizational recognition through artifacts, beliefs, values, and positive assumptions about what career success can mean to different people such as being climbers, experts, influencers, and self-realizers, and how this gratification should be respected. Climbers are described as those who define success as climbing up the professional hierarchy ladder, experts who enjoy success in achieving competence in their jobs and being recognized personally for being good, influencers for whom success is defined as being able to do things that had a clear and positive effect, whatever their hierarchical position is, and self-realizers for whom success is based on achievement on their terms for personal fulfillment, with a balance between work and home life. If the company's policies and practices recognize this, it will propel toward the path of success. Dual career ladders are an excellent vehicle for those talents who are not keen on the traditional management growth ladder.

On a side note, to motivate individuals to pursue their interests, it will not be a bad idea for HR to go back to its schoolbook principle model of Hertzberg's Hygiene-Motivation, which reinstates the importance of intrinsic motivation over extrinsic motivation. Apart from basic hygiene factors being taken care of, individuals can be motivated intrinsically through a sense of meaning and purpose, a sense of competence, a sense of choice, and a sense of progression. All of these contribute significantly to creating value for self and the organization.

Fourth,

An organizational culture that fosters continuous learning and develops leadership qualities from the early stages of careers can make a huge difference. One way of doing this can be through distributive, collective, or shared leadership concepts. Distributed leadership is not something 'done' by an individual 'to' others, or a set of individual actions through which people contribute to a group or organization. It is a group activity that works through and within relationships, rather than individual action. This can work well in contemporary knowledge-based organizations where the work is complex and must be coordinated between multiple project teams. Because individuals and young project managers will face situations that require them to showcase their leadership qualities, leadership attributes can be developed among junior and middle management through a fluid and emergent social process, while also learning from one's own mistakes and those of others.

For this to happen real, organizations' should embrace innovative features such as hierarchy being less authoritative but more distributed, division of labor is less specialization in the job but more expanded job roles, the rule is more discretionary and relationship-based, and system directed towards change and rewards oriented towards group performance. Of course, all of this is only possible with the right policies and practices and human resources have an essential role in designing the same.

Fifth, coaching and mentoring for continuous personal and professional development in becoming a Leader.

The thing about the organizational situation is that it can be unique every time and that is the beauty of it. Blake-Mouton through his behavioral theory[92] described how leaders could influence group members through certain behavior. He reinstated the need to be a Team Leader, which is a highly ideal combination of task and people concern. Hersey and Blanchard's Situational Leadership[93] taught us how we could master situations with the right leadership approach such as Telling, Selling, Participating, and Delegating. It is an effective way to manage and lead teams for effective outcomes based on team members' willingness and ability levels. Max Landsberg complimented this through skill/will matrix,[94] a practical coaching approach a leader might take. Fiedler's contingency theory[95] took another route stating that we do not have to change our leadership styles based on situations instead we can change the situations for effective outcomes. Known as situational favorableness, it encouraged a change in the situation through leader-member relations, power, and task structure. Path goal theory[96] illustrated the way a leader in removing obstacles on his way. The fact of the matter is there is no size-fit solution. Every time a leader can be unique and can present something new and exciting. As I mentioned earlier, that is the beauty of it and perhaps the best way would be to leave it to the individual's judgment to perform the role

---

[92] Blake, R. R., & Mouton, S.J., (1964), The Managerial Grid, Gulf Publishing Company.

[93] Blanchard, H.K., & Hersey, P., (1982), Management of Organizational Behavior - Utilizing Human Resources, Prentice-Hall.

[94] Landsber, M., (1996), The Toa of coaching, Profile Books.

[95] Fiedler, E.F., (1963), A Contingency Model of Leadership Effectiveness, Group Effectiveness Research Laboratory, University of Illinois.

[96] House, R. J. (1971). A Path Goal Theory of Leader Effectiveness. Administrative Science Quarterly, 16, 321-339. Sage Publications. https://doi.org/10.2307/2391905.

of a leader, given the task, situation, and other considerations. That being the case, it would be of paramount importance for Leaders to be coached and mentored to unleash their fullest potential for peak performance.

The best way to do this would be to invest in continuous personal and professional development. The International Coaching Federation offers a range of professional coaching certifications to all aspirants. The best things about such programs are that they train you to coach others and develop you as a leader in that due course. Such concepts should be complemented by policies that go hand in hand to provide the right skill developmental programs. To quote, Continuous Professional Development should be mandatory for all junior and middle management. We can be creative and make 10% of the individual CTC linked to Continuous Professional Development and extend 10% from their end outside the CTC in the form of a Human Capital Development policy. From an organizational design and structure aspect, Holocracy[97] is a practical way to allow individuals to experiment with leadership attributes in real time. Our responsibility is to have such models exercise autonomy and discretion that facilitates decision-making and leadership. The more significant point is we prepare young managers to develop leadership competence through suitable support systems to align with the company's mission and vision.

For all the above 5 practices, we need a positive, trustworthy culture that encourages them to 'Experiment'. First-time mistakes are acceptable as long as they are not repeated and present an opportunity to promote innovation. At the core of such a culture building would be RESPECT.

We spoke about Innovation and Disruptive Innovation in Slide 2. But only that would be possible if a culture of trust is built within the organization. I keep returning to the subject of Trust as it is the basic

---

[97] Robertson, J, B., (2015), Holacracy - The New Management System for a Rapidly Changing World, Henry Holt and Company.

core of any successful enterprise. If an organization is not built on the foundation of Trust then it is Trash!

Let me now tell you about my philosophy of management. Broadly, I believe, 'People work for their supervisors either out of Fear or Respect'. Mind you, I am not talking about their internal drives but about their external influence. I know I can speak confidently for this group, we all want our team members to work out of respect for us. But at the same time, we are also discussing the need to embrace Servant Leadership. We as Leaders need to ensure that our team members do not perceive such a leadership style as weak. As leaders, we must exhibit behaviors and attributes that will replace 'Fear' with 'Respect'.

Respect in our dictionary should read as Respect for every individual, Respect for the profession, Respect for the mission and the vision of the organization, and, importantly Respect for the individual's commitment, including self, and towards the goals and objectives. 'Respect' is so directly proportional to trust, building innovative culture, coping with change, and most of all, being human. You can create such a mindset only if you exhibit it in your behavior and action. All of these will be a rewarding experience both for the employees and the management. This brings me to the next aspect of the people practice and I would like to propose Rewards!'

'Did we just not speak about Rewards extensively in Slide 4?' asked Krish.

Pabloo continued, 'We did! But through this People practice slide, I would like to recommend best practices. Again, as Shiva mentioned, tie it back to the organization with specific policies around it. First and foremost, our Rewards strategy should have a two-fold approach. The first is the basic essential compensation and perks factors that get us on level with the market. The second is to promote pay for performance. The basic essential is non-negotiable, and we must be at par with the industry. An effective way to arrive at our compensation would be to take support from specific agencies with expertise and benchmark our compensation. Additionally, it is crucial to undertake weighted surveys. 'Weighted surveys' are typically among companies within the industry, this in turn increases the accuracy driven by data.

Now, based on this survey report, we should build our basic essential compensation philosophy. By philosophy, I mean the identification of our pay policy. This strategic approach will influence both employee attraction and retention. The strategy can be different for different areas of the organization. For example, we can broadly divide the pay policy for the organization into junior, middle, and senior segments. This approach of weighted surveys can make a huge difference, especially in the junior and middle segments. Typically, we can choose our pay policy among a Lead Policy, a Lag Policy, or a Match policy.

Lead Policy is an approach where we project how the other companies' pay scale will be at the end of the structure year and exceed those rates. By doing so, we will lead the market. Such an approach will support any aggressive growth plan by attracting large-scale hiring. The Lag policy can be chosen if we want to be cost-conscious and do not have any large scaling. Basically, we will project where the market will be at the start of the year and we will lag the market. Finally, match policy is a balanced approach where we project the market will be in the middle of the structured year. Based on it, we will lead the market for the first six months and lag it for the next six months. Such an approach can be beneficial in a dynamic market, especially in a tight labor market, as we can ensure our pay scale remains competitive through a catch-up.

A lot of factors have to be considered before we arrive at a pay policy for our organization. This is important as close to 90% of our workforce are at the junior and middle management level and the payroll cost is the single most significant and highest cost from an overheads standpoint. This means a complete alignment is needed between the goals of the company and the pay policy. The direction of the senior management and the board members is very critical to this decision.

Krish raised a point, 'Is it not always best for us to take a lag policy? This way, we will avert any risk and allow the market to take its course and then take our decisions.'

Pabloo responded, 'it is an approach but not necessarily the best one. Suppose, if we do take that approach, then it gives our competitors a position to start poaching our talents with lucrative salaries and this means we will have an attrition problem at hand. The cost of attrition alone can have a grave effect on the organization's sustainability. We need to remember here the word 'cost' is not just the quantifiable number but also the loss of tenured employees. We earlier discussed RBVF as an advantage, and if we lose talents, we will retrograde. The key here would be to take not just a balanced approach but also a customized approach. For example, we can choose a reward policy that is different from each other among the junior, middle, and senior management. The junior or entry-level pay policy should be competitive and maybe through a lead policy we can address the needs of the young demographic with spot awards and career progression. This will support our growth plans and expansion. For the middle management, the approach can be a match policy with a lot of focus on pay for performance and professional development sponsorship. The Lag policy might sound like a disadvantage to the senior management. Still, the winning combination can be to keep the base pay minimal and bonuses and long-term incentives to the maximum. Of course, long-term benefits such as stock options, deferred compensation, executive perks, and benefits should be tied up to the executive's performance and the organization's growth.

As I mentioned earlier, alignment with the company's mission and vision is the key to arriving at our total rewards compensation and philosophy. In fact, what we discuss here may not necessarily work as everything is situational. We need to consider STEEPLE and CLIPS for many of our business decisions. We did speak about it in Slovakia. STEEPLE is an acronym for Socio-cultural, Technological, Economic, Environmental, Political, Legal, and Ethical and CLIPS is an acronym for Culture, Layout, Innovation, Power, and Social components of the organization. All our people's policies should revolve around this and we should create a compelling employee value proposition that is different, credible and sustainable. By various means, the first consideration is how we make our organization different from the others and whether we are clear about our organization's attributes that attract, retain and motivate talents. By Credible, our organizational attributes should be real, pervasive and not aspired. In other words, it should be a real-time execution of those attributes. Lastly, by sustainable, our employee value propositions should not be at risk and become vulnerable to the market conditions in the competitive landscape. This leadership has to drive these factors until it becomes the organization's DNA.'

The Last Slide:
Do We Dare to Make a Difference?

Pabloo in a confident voice added, 'My last slide, in many ways, is the first starting point for an organization that differentiates itself from the rest. The first thing that strikes the eyes of all stakeholders, irrespective of internal and external, is an organization's brand. So much a cliché, but as they say, the first impression is always the best. The best way to understand employment branding would be through an example: McDonald - When the organization had its first quarterly loss in 47 years of operation, it began the development of a revitalization plan. Part of the plan was creating the "My First" campaign highlighting that many of its top executives started their career success by working at the restaurants. In addition, the recruiters and all their recruitment materials emphasized the extraordinary career opportunities at McDonald's. All this added to the employment brand becoming an organization focused on building skills and instilling pride in its employees.[98]

'It was beautifully quoted, "if the reputation of a company's products are services is its face, the talent brand is its heart and soul"[99] If we have to be a unique brand, we must craft our talent brand! A talent brand is a personification of what it means to be a member of a particular organization and how others positively describe it. Again, there are

---

[98] Marguez, J (2006). When brand alone is not enough. Workforce management, 39-41.

[99] Rueff, R., and Stringer, H. (2006). Talent force: A new manifesto for the human side of business. Upper Saddle River, NJ; Prentice Hall.

many success stories of an organization that builds a unique talent brand for themselves, such as, Google has built its reputation on innovation and risk-taking ability. Its talent brand is young, intelligent and full of free-thinking. On the other hand, Microsoft has built its reputation on a single-minded focus on market domination. Its talent brand is smart; it has highly competitive people with unbridled work ethics. Likewise, we need to craft our unique talent brand to characterize our organization. Every time we converse or engage with anyone is an opportunity for us to showcase our brand and make an impression! I am talking about opportunities for us to craft our talent brand outside the traditional brand-building activities such as Prints, PR activities, Ads, Social media campaigns, etc. All of it has become essential for any organization to be in the business world. But to differentiate, we need to add the human touch.'

'I like this' mentioned Singh enthusiastically and added, 'Pabloo, tell us how can the leaders in this room contribute to this effect?'

'A good starting point for the leaders in this room is to begin crafting their own leadership brand!' continued Pabloo, 'Just as talent brand is the personification of what it means to be part of the organization, leadership is the personification of the consistent traits and behavior of the leaders of the organization[100]. As mentioned earlier, many organizations have realized this through their leadership brand. Going back to the Microsoft example, the leaders in the organization are known for their attributes of high intelligence, a desire to dominate competitors, and high technical competence. From our organization context, we need to deliberate and realize the benefits the leadership brand can bring to the organization. We need to connect our organizational strategy and culture to the behaviors the leaders must exhibit. To us and others, it should describe the kind of leaders who

---

[100] Ulrich, D., and Smallwood, N. (2007). Leadership brand: Developing cutomer focused leaders to drive performance and build lasting value. Boston: Harvard Business School Press.

make the organization successful and the shared identity that separates our leadership from the competition. As leaders, we need to inculcate a behavior that shapes the success of the organization. The beauty of crafting such leadership brands is that it does not require any advertising. Since it is genuine and authentic, the talent brand will craft itself eventually through culture and image. This is not something that can happen overnight. It requires dedication, zeal, and a true spirit to make a difference!' explained Pabloo.

He continued with utmost excitement and strength and a smile, 'So... Are we ready to begin the journey? As leaders, are we willing to take ownership to excel? Are we committed to our organizational goals? Are we going to walk the talk? And lastly, Do we dare to make a difference?

'YES!' was the unquestionable response Pabloo received with tremendous applause! Singh walked up to Pabloo, shook his hands, and said, 'impressive! As the organization's CEO, I always believe the first and foremost job of a Human Resource professional is to motivate, harness, and channel the employees' energy toward the organizational objectives. You have succeeded in leading and inspiring us toward a greater future! I am taking away a lot of positives from your presentation. I understand that we have to work on the finer details, but this session has oriented us with a direction for all of the leaders. Now the onus is on us to steer this forward. That being said, I want you to champion this project journey from good to great!'

'Thank you, Singh!' mentioned Pabloo with a sense of accomplishment. 'I should say all of the ideas in the presentation were pieces of information that I have borrowed from renowned HR scholars and Management leaders. If anything, they deserve all the accolades for their relentless efforts to make the world a better workplace! I am just thankful for being allowed to showcase their brilliance through this presentation. Also, I am very excited about the opportunity to champion this project journey. I can say with absolute confidence that we will make the organization good to great, thanks to this diverse group of knowledgeable senior leaders embracing and welcoming change and new initiatives.'

'I also want to thank the senior leaders for all their support in making this presentation. Together, we encouraged ourselves to be open and transparent and move out of our comfort zones. We kept telling ourselves that we would not shy away from our challenges and it was fine to go into uncomfortable territory seeking answers for our real-time problems. We are motivated to address the true cause of our problems and determined to drive for success. We will don many hats, such as Coach, Influencer, Business partner, Mentor, Intrapreneur, Leader, Change Agent, and Challenger, exhibiting curiosity to learn things and enjoy success with a spirit of celebration. As we embark on this journey, we promise to be ethical in our approach and being. Our interest will not alone be with the organization's success but also to make a successful community and have a communitarian view of the firm rather than a stockholder one. Business ethics will be central to all the judgments and decisions we make and in designing socially responsible practices and exhibit key attributes, including humility, authenticity, and a willingness to put the needs of the employees, the institution, and the society! As leaders, we will continuously influence to build it as our culture! As a unit, we stay committed, and as individuals, we will be open to learning and keep upskilling ourselves to reach new levels of leadership.'

'We will don many hats'

'Right now, I'm reminded of a story I have heard. There was a woodcutter who asked a timber merchant for a job. The woodcutter had the skills required to cut trees and the timber merchant took him to the forest and offered him good pay for every tree he chopped. The woodcutter impressed the timber merchant by cutting many trees daily. The timber merchant rewarded the woodcutter as agreed. In the initial days, both the woodcutter and the timber merchant were very happy as the woodcutter got paid well, thanks to his skills in cutting many trees, and the timber merchant in finding an efficient worker. However, as days progressed, there was a dip in the number of trees the woodcutter chopped. No matter how hard he tried, he could never cut the same number of trees as before. The woodcutter thought he was losing his strength and eventually walked up to the timber merchant and mentioned he could no longer chop the trees as he once did. The timber merchant tried convincing him otherwise, but the words alone could not get the woodcutter to his earlier proven skill.

Many of you would know this story and the mistake the woodcutter and the timber merchant made. Unfortunately, both of them were so engrossed in their world that they forgot to sharpen the Axe!

Singh, today we promise to sharpen our Axe in this journey. We will not be complacent with our initial success but strive for sustainability in everything we do. Driven by purpose, we will equip ourselves and the people around us in this journey, and together, we will dare to make a difference!'

LET US BEGIN!

Bibliography

S.no	References/Citations
1	David E. Guest, Neil Conway (2002), Human Resource Management Journal. Wiley Online Library
2	Boxall, P and Purcell, J (2003), Strategic Human Resource Management, Palgrave Macmillan, Basingstoke
3	Beer, M., et al. (1985). Managing human assets. Personnel Administrator, 30(3), 74–81
4	Purcell, J., Kinnie, N., Hutchinson, S., Rayton, B., & Swart, J. (2003). Understanding the people and performance link: Unlocking the black box. London: CIPD.
5	Pfeffer,J (1998) The Human Equation: Building Profits by Putting People First, Harvard Business School Press.
6	Schein, E (2010) Organizational Culture and Leadership (The Jossey–Bass Business & Management Series), John Wiley & Sons.
7	Edgar, D., & Stonehouse, G., (2011), Business Strategy: An Introduction, Third Edition, Quote Page 263, Palgrave Macmillan, London.
8	Deal, T. and Kennedy, A. (1982) Corporate Cultures, Basic Books.
9	Srivatsva, S., Cooperrider, D., (1999) Appreciative Management and Leadership, The power of positive Thought and Action in Organizations, Williams Custom.
10	Farnham, D., (2015) Human Resource Management in Context, Kogan Page.

S.no	References/Citations
11	Farnham, D., (2015) Human Resource Management in Context, Kogan Page.
12	Wolf, M., (2000) Stepping Stone from Poverty and the big lie of global inequality, Financial Times.
13	Birdall,N., (2005). Rising Inequility in the New Global Economy, University of California, Berkley, World Institute for Development Economics Research.
14	Bower, J. and Christensen, C., (1995), Disruptive Technologies: Catching the wave, Harvard Business School Pub
15	Jennings, C., (2013), 70:20:10 Framework Explained, Creating High Performance Cultures, Forum Pty Limited
16	Strauss, W. and Howe, N., (1997), The Fourth Turning, What the cycles of History Tell Us About America's Next Rendezvous with Destiny, Crown
17	Harjani, A., (2014), From brats to bosses – Gen Y to dominated by 2025. https://www.cnbc.com/2014/01/22/to-bosses--gen-y-to-dominate-by-2025.html
18	European Commission, (2002), Commission welcomes political agreement on Gender Balance on Corporate Boards. https://ec.europa.eu/commission/presscorner/detail/en/IP_22_3478
19	Butler,T.,"Hiring an Entrepreneurial Leader: What to Look For." Harvard Business Review 95, no. 2 (March–April 2017): 85–93
20	Kruger, J., & Dunning, D. (1999). Unskilled and unaware of it: How difficulties in recognizing one's own incompetence lead to inflated self-assessments. Journal of Personality and Social Psychology, 77(6), 1121–1134. https://doi.org/10.1037/0022-3514.77.6.1121
21	Cooperrider, D., Whitney, D., (2005), Appreciative Enquiry – A positive revolution in Change, Berrett-Koehler Publishers

S.no	References/Citations
22	Hofstede, G., (2001), Culture's Consequences – Comparing Values, Behaviors, Institution and Organizations Across Nations, SAGE Publications
23	State of The Global Workplace, (2017), Gallup Press.
24	Chalofsky, N.,and Krishna, V., (2009), Meaningfulness, commitment and engagement: The intersection of a deeper level of intrinsic motivation, Advances in Developing Human Resources. 11,189-203
25	Morris, S., and Snell, S., (2009), The evolution of HR strategy: adaptations in increasing global complexity. The SAGE handbook of human resource management
26	Ulrich, D. and Brockbank, W., (2005), The HR value proposition, Boston: Harvard Business School Press
27	Argyris, C. & Schon, D. (1978). Organizational Learning: A Theory of Action Perspective. Reading, Massachusetts: Addison-Wesley Publishing Co. & Mezirow, J. (1991). Transformative dimensions in adult learning. San Francisco: Jossey-Bass
28	Berne,E., (1961), Transactional Analysis in Psychotherapy A Systematic Individual and Social Psychiatry, Souvenir Press
29	Pettigrew, A., (1973), The politics of Organizational decision-making, Tavistock
30	Pfeffer, J., (2022), 7 Rules of Power – Surprising – But True – Advice on how to get things done and Advance your career, Swift Press
31	Mayer, J., Brackett, M., & Salovey, P., (2004), Emotional Intelligence, Dude Pub
32	Drake, D., Spence, G., & Bachkirova, T., (2016), The SAGE Handbook of Coaching, SAGE Publications
33	Whitmore, J., (1993), Coaching for Performance – A Practical guide for Growing your Own Business, John Wiley & Sons

S.no	References/Citations
34	Murphy, W.M., (2012), Reverse mentoring at work: Fostering cross-generational learning and developing millennial leaders, Wiley online library, Citations: 144.
35	Tannenbaum, A. S., & Georgopoulos, B. S. (1957). The distribution of control in formal organizations. Social Forces, 36, 44–50.
36	Boxall, P.F., and Purcell, J. (2003), Strategy and Human Resource Management, Palgrave Macmillan
37	Morris, J., Blyton, P., (1991), A Flexible Future? - Prospects for Employment and Organization, de Gruyter
38	Maslow, H.A., (1981), Motivation And Personality, Harper & Row
39	Adams, J. S. (1963). Towards an understanding of inequity. The Journal of Abnormal and Social Psychology, 67(5), 422–436.
40	Herzberg, F., (1968), One more time - How do you motivate Employees, Harvard Business Review & Maslow, A. H. (1943). A theory of human motivation. Psychological Review, 50, 370–396.
41	Palmer, T. M., & Barnett, A.G., (1998), Mutual Influence in Interpersonal Communication Theory and Research in Cognition, Affect, and Behavior, Ablex Publishing Corporation.
42	Greenhaus, J., & Callanan, G. (1994), Career management, Fort Worth: Dryden
43	Woollams, S., & Brown, M., (1978), Transactional Analysis. MIcooper: Stan Woollams.
44	Landsberg, M., (1997) The Tao of Coaching - Boost Your Effectiveness at Work by Inspiring and Developing Those Around You. (Santa Monica, CA: Knowledge Exchange, 1997).

S.no	References/Citations
45	Vygotsky, L. S. (1978). Mind in society: The development of higher psychological processes Cambridge, Mass.: Harvard University Press
46	Parker, P., Hall, D. T., & Kram, K. E. (2008). Peer coaching: A relational process for accelerating career learning. Academy of Management Learning & Education, 7, 487-503
47	Kaptein, M. & Wempe, J., (1998), The Ethics Report: A means of sharing responsibility, Business Ethics A European Review 7(3):131-139
48	Lawton, A. (1999), Ethics and Management. In A. Rose & A.Lawton (Eds.), Public service management (pp.299-300), Harlow, UK:Prentice Hall
49	Ulrich, D., (1997), Human Resource Champions: The next agenda for adding value and delivering results. Harvard Business Press, Cambridge, MA, ISBN: 9780875847191, Pages: 281
50	Bhaduri,N.S. & Selarka, E. (2016), Corporate Governance and Corporate Social Responsibility of Indian Companies, Springer Singapore (ebook)
51	Gabaix, X. & Landier, A. (2008), Why has CEO pay increased so much? Quarterly Journal of Economics 123 (1): 49-100.
52	Aguilar, F.J., (1967), Scanning the business Enviornment, 1st ed. New York, Macmillan company
53	Hofstede, G. (1991). Cultures and Organizations: Software of the Mind. London, UK: McGraw-Hill & Hofstede, G., Hofstede, G.J., Hofstede, M., (2010), "Cultures and Organizations, Software of the Mind", Third Revised Edition, McGraw-Hill.
54	Riso, D.R., and Hudson, R., (1999) The Wisdom of the Enneagram: The Complete Guide to Psychological and Spiritual Growth for the Nine Personality Types, Bantam Books.

S.no	References/Citations
55	Myers, I.B., (1998), MBTI Manual - A Guide to the Development and Use of the Myers-Briggs Type Indicator, Consulting Psychologists Press.
56	Brickner, M. A., Harkins, S. G., & Ostrom, T. M. (1986). Effects of personal involvement: Thought-provoking implications for social loafing. Journal of Personality and Social Psychology,51(4), 763-769.
57	Kerr, N.L., & Brunn, S.E.,(1981), Ringelmann Revisited: Alternative Explanations for the Social Loafing Effect, First Published, Research Article, https://doi.org/10.1177/014616728172007
58	Giang, V. (2013). The 'two pizza rule' is Jeff Bezos' secret to productive meetings. Business Insider. Retrieved from www.businessinsider.com/jeff-bezos-two-pizza-rule-for-productive-meetings-2013-10
59	Engelhardt, A. (2006): The 3/2 rule of employee productivity. CYBAEA Journal, http://www.cybaea.net/Blogs/Journal/employee_productivity.html (accessed: January, 2013).
60	Pinchot, G., (1985) Intrapreneuring: Why You Don't Have to Leave the Corporation to Become an Entrepreneur, Harper & Row
61	Christensen, C.M., (2016), The Clayton M. Christensen Reader, Harvard Business Review Press & Christensen, C.M.,Raynor, M.E., Gregersen, H., (2011) Disruptive Innovation: The Christensen Collection (The Innovator's Dilemma, The Innovator's Solution, The Innovator's DNA, and Harvard Business Review Article "How Will You Measure Your Life?"), Harvard Business Review Press.
62	Nonaka, I., Toyama, R. and Konno, N. (2000). 'SECI, Ba, and leadership: a unified model of dynamic knowledge creation'. Long Range Planning.

S.no	References/Citations
63	Moore, E.G., & Moore, E.G., "Cramming More Components Onto Integrated Circuits", Electronics Magazine, vol. 38, no. 8, pp. 114-117, April 1965
64	Kurzweil, R., (2000), The Age of Spiritual Machines - When Computers Exceed Human Intelligence, Penguin Publishing Group
65	Grey, C. (2005) A very short, fairly interesting and reasonable cheap book about studying organizations, Sage: London
66	Allio, R. J. (2008a). C. K. Prahalad heralds a new era of innovation. Strategy & Leadership, 36(6),11-14. doi: 10.1108/10878570810918304
67	Coch, L., & French, J. R. P., Jr. (1948). Overcoming resistance to change. Human Relations, 1, 512–532. https://doi.org/10.1177/001872674800100408
68	M. Crossan, H.W. Lane, R.E. White, An organizational learning framework: From intuition to institution, Academy of Management Review, 24 (1999), pp. 522-537
69	Rousseau, D.M., S. Sitkin, R.S. Burt and C. Camerer (1998), 'Not so different after all: A cross-discipline view of trust', Academy of Management Review, 23, 393–404.
70	Bateman, T.S., & Organ, D.W., (1983), Job satisfaction and the good solider: The relationship between affect and employee "citizenship". Academy of Management Journal, 26, 587-595.
71	Holbeche,L.S., Matthews,G., (2012), Engaged: unleashing the potential of your organisation through employee engagement, John Wiley/Jossey Bass.
72	Vroom, V.H., & Deci, E.L., (1972), Management and Motivation - Selected Readings, Penguin Education.
73	Nohria, N., & Groysberg, B., (2008), Employee Motivation: A powerful new model, Harvard Business Review 86(7-8):78-84, 160

S.no	References/Citations
74	Michael,H., & Minor,D., (2016), "Workplace Design: The Good, the Bad, and the Productive." Harvard Business School Working Paper, No. 16-147.
75	Meyer, H.H., Kay, E., & French, J.R.P., (1965), Split roles in performance appraisal. Harvard Business Review, 43 (1), 129-142
76	DeNesi, A.S., & Kluger, A., (2000), Feedback effectiveness: Can 360-degree appraisals be improved? Academy of Management Perspectives 14(1):129-139
77	Toquam, L, J., (1988), Development and Field Test of Behaviorally Anchored Rating Scales for Nine MOS, U.S. Army Research Institute for the Behavioral and Social Sciences, University of Minnesota.
78	Latham, P.G., & Wexley, N.K., (1977), Behavioral Observation Scales for Performance Appraisal Purposes, Wiley Online Library, Citations: 123
79	VandeWalle, D., & Cummings, L. L. (1997). A test of the influence of goal orientation on the feedback-seeking process. Journal of Applied Psychology, 82(3), 390–400
80	Clegg, S.R., Kornberger, M., Pitsis, T., (2011), Managing and Organizations - An Introduction to Theory and Practice, SAGE Publications.
81	Johnson, W.M., & Suskewicz, J., (2020), Lead from the Future - How to Turn Visionary Thinking Into Breakthrough Growth, Harvard Business Review Press. O'Leonard, K., & Krider, J., (2014), Leadership development facebook 2014: Benchmarks and trends in U.S Leadership development, Bersin by Deloitte.
82	Greenleaf, R. K., Frick, D.M., & Spears, L.C., (1996) On Becoming a Servant Leader - The Private Writings of Robert K. Greenleaf, Wiley.

S.no	References/Citations
83	Peterson, L., & Felfe, J., (2007), Romance of Leadership and management decision making, European Journal of Work and Organizational Psychology, 16:1, 1-24, https://doi.org/10.1080/13594320600873076
84	Barney, J. (1991) Firm Resources and Sustained Competitive Advantage. Journal of Management, 17, 99-120
85	Barney,J. (1995). Looking Inside for Competitive Advantage. Academy of Management Executive, 9(4), pp. 49-61
86	Gay, M., & Sims, D., (2007) Building Tomorrow's Talent: A Practitioner's Guide to Talent Management and Sucession Planning, Author House.
87	Peter, J.L., & Hull, R., (1969) The Peter Principal, Harper Collins
88	Jennings, C., (2013), 70:20:10 Framework Explained, Creating High Performance Cultures, Forum Pty Limited, Center for Creative Leadership. (n.d.), The 70-20-10 rule of leadership development. Retrieved https://www.ccl.org/articles/leading-effectively-articles/70-20-10-rule/
89	The real Peter Principle: promotion to pain. Harvard Business Review - Hess, H. H. (1976)
90	John, E.F., Schuerger, J.M., & Watterson, D.G., (1980), Personality measures as predictors of managerial performance and salaries. Paper presented at the meeting of the Midwest Soceity for Multivariate Experimental Psychology, St. Louis, MO.
91	Goleman, D., (2006), Emotional Intelligence - Why It Can Matter More Than IQ. Random House Publishing Group.
92	Blake, R. R., & Mouton, S.J., (1964), The Managerial Grid, Gulf Publishing Company
93	Blanchard, H.K., & Hersey, P., (1982), Management of Organizational Behavior - Utilizing Human Resources, Prentice-Hall.

S.no	References/Citations
94	Landsber, M., (1996), The Toa of coaching, Profile Books
95	Fiedler, E.F., (1963), A Contingency Model of Leadership Effectiveness, Group Effectiveness Research Laboratory, University of Illinois
96	House, R. J. (1971). A Path Goal Theory of Leader Effectiveness. Administrative Science Quarterly, 16, 321-339. Sage Publications. https://doi.org/10.2307/2391905
97	Robertson, J, B., (2015), Holacracy - The New Management System for a Rapidly Changing World, Henry Holt and Company
98	Marguez, J (2006). When brand alone is not enough. Workforce management, 39-41.
99	Rueff, R., and Stringer, H. (2006). Talent force: A new manifesto for the human side of business. Upper Saddle River, NJ; Prentice Hall.
100	Ulrich, D., and Smallwood, N. (2007). Leadership brand: Developing cutomer focused leaders to drive performance and build lasting value. Boston: Harvard Business School Press